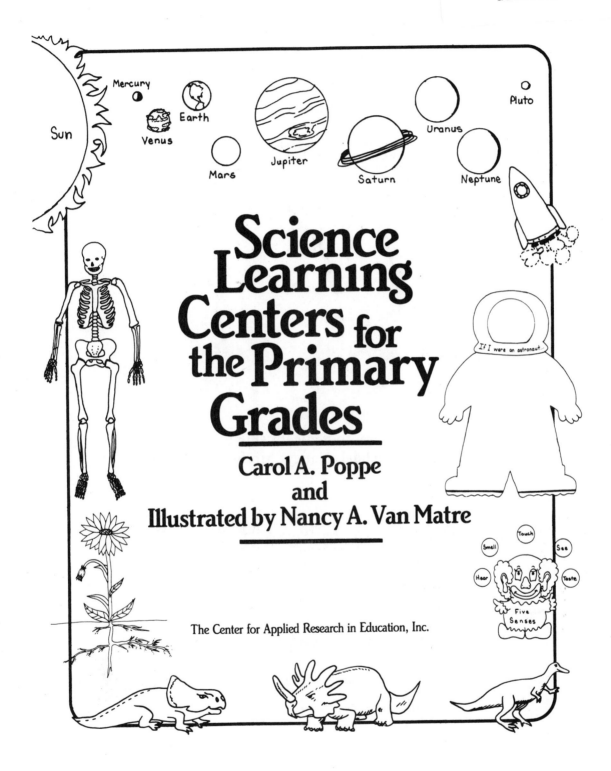

Science Learning Centers for the Primary Grades

Carol A. Poppe
and
Illustrated by Nancy A. Van Matre

The Center for Applied Research in Education, Inc.

10 9 8 7

We wish to dedicate this book to
Jason, Michael, Nancy, Molly, and Jenny

Library of Congress Cataloging in Publication Data

Poppe, Carol A.
  Science learning centers for the primary grades.

  1. Science—Study and teaching (Primary)
2. Classroom learning centers—Planning.   3. Activity
programs in education.   I. Van Matre, Nancy A.
II. Title.
LB1532.P67   1985   372.3'5044   85-13284

ISBN 0-87628-749-6

About the Authors

CAROL A. POPPE received her B.A. degree from Ohio University and has taken several graduate courses at Oakland University and Siena Heights College. Mrs. Poppe has 20 years of teaching experience at the first- and second-grade levels.

NANCY A. VAN MATRE received her B.A. degree from Eastern Michigan University, and her M.A. degree in Reading. She has been actively teaching grades one through three for more than nine years.

Both authors have presented several learning center workshops for other educators in Michigan and Ohio, and are currently teaching first grade in the Clinton Community Schools in Clinton, Michigan. Learning center activities have been an integral part of their daily classroom schedules since 1976.

About This Book

Science Learning Centers for the Primary Grades is designed to help the primary teacher develop and organize a system in which each child participates daily at an individual learning center.

Specific techniques are given to help you effectively manage a learning center system as an integral part of the day's activities. One example is the Color Wheel, which controls the child's movement among four work areas: learning centers, reading, seatwork, and boardwork.

In addition, a variety of methods are provided to help you arrange the classroom environment to incorporate learning centers. Ideas for developing, introducing, setting up, and evaluating learning centers are suggested for easy use. Innovative approaches that encourage parent involvement, both in the classroom and at home, are also given.

Five science learning center units are provided, each containing eight learning center activities based on a particular science theme, including

- The Five Senses
- The Human Body
- Space
- Plants
- Dinosaurs

The learning center activities provide each child with a variety of opportunities to learn something new, to reinforce previously taught concepts, and to develop creativity. During an eight-day period, every child has a chance to complete all eight activities in a given unit.

The ideas and activities presented in this book are designed for use by the primary teacher, as well as resource-room teachers and teachers of special education classes. The units are appropriate for students in kindergarten through third grade, and are useful for students at all developmental levels. The science learning center units teach and reinforce the skills presented in the table.

Each set of directions for the science learning center units combines illustrations with simple sentences to enable virtually every child to complete the activities independently.

Among the many special features of this book are the practical, ready-to-use ideas and reproducible materials that will help you develop and use the 40 science learning center activities. Each of the learning center units contains

- Reproducible illustrated direction pages designed for mounting on file folders.

Skills

Science Learning Center Units	Classifying	Communicating	Creating	Creative Writing	Experimenting	Fine-Motor Coordination	Listening	Map-reading	Matching	Measuring	Observing	Perception	Predicting	Using Reference Materials	Sorting
The five senses	x	x	x	x		x	x		x		x	x		x	x
The human body		x	x			x	x			x	x			x	
Space		x	x	x		x	x	x	x	x	x		x		
Plants	x	x	x	x	x	x	x		x	x	x				x
Dinosaurs	x		x	x	x	x	x		x	x	x				x

- Reproducible full-page student activity pages.
- An illustrated bulletin-board activity.
- A letter to parents explaining the learning center activities and suggesting home enrichment ideas.
- A group activity that can be done by the entire class or a smaller group.
- Boardwork for related theme activities.
- A reproducible learning center marker for each student.
- A reproducible master list of the eight learning center activities to be used as a reference in a lesson plan book, materials storage box, and so on.
- Eight related learning center theme activities from the content areas of art, handwriting, math, geography, reading, science, and spelling. In each unit one of the eight activities is open-ended, so that any skill you wish to emphasize may be adapted for the learning center activity.

The following list of resources will help you develop additional ideas for learning centers.

Borba, Craig and Michele Borba. *The Good Apple Guide to Learning Centers.* Carthage, IL: Good Apple, Inc., 1978.

Davidson, Tom and Judy Steely. *Using Learning Centers with Not-Yet Readers.* Santa Monica, CA: Goodyear Publishing Co., 1978.

Kaplan, Sandra N., Jo Ann B. Kaplan, Sheila K. Madsen, and Bette Taylor Gould. *A Young Child Experiences.* Pacific Palisades, CA: Goodyear Publishing Co., 1975.

Kaplan, Sandra N., Jo Ann B. Kaplan, Sheila K. Madsen, and Bette K. Taylor. *Change for Children*. Pacific Palisades, CA: Goodyear Publishing Co., 1973.

Lorton, Mary B. *Work Jobs*. Menlo Park, CA: Addison-Wesley Publishing Co., 1972.

Waynant, Louise F. *Learning Centers II . . . Practical Ideas for You*. New York: McGraw-Hill, 1977.

With this book you can make learning centers an important part of your teaching program to help develop independent learners. The materials offered here will guide you in reaching that goal.

Carol A. Poppe

Nancy A. Van Matre

To the Teacher

The directions for each of the science learning centers in this book are designed to fit on 12-by-18-inch file folders. Bright-colored file folders are attractive and suitable for this purpose; a glue stick works well for mounting the direction pages. Crayons or water-based marking pens may be used to color the pictures and numbers. (Prior to mounting any directions, be sure the other side of the page has been duplicated for future use.)

How to make the direction file folder:

1. Glue the Teacher Directions to the back of the file folder. (This visual aid is helpful to you in organizing the necessary materials for the learning center.)

2. Glue the Directions for File Folder Activities to the adjacent side of the file folder, as shown in the illustration.

3. Color the pictures on the student file folder directions page.

4. Color the numbers orange on the student file folder directions page. (Use the same format for all of the file folders.)

5. Glue the student file folder directions page to the inside of the file folder. (See the illustration.)

6. Laminate or use clear self-stick vinyl to cover all of the direction file folders.

Optional ideas for making direction file folders:

1. Additional theme pictures from magazines, catalogs, and old textbooks may be glued to the side adjacent to the student file folder directions page.

2. A 10-by-13-inch envelope with a student activity page mounted on it may be attached to the side adjacent to the student file folder directions page. The envelope is used to hold the student activity page.

Direction file folder tip for the nonreader or beginning reader:

Make a set of corresponding file folder directions numbers on 1-inch squares of orange construction paper with a black marking pen. Staple or tape these numbers to the student activity page container, books, tape recorder, games, and so on, at the learning center. The numbers assist the student with less-developed reading skills to complete the activities in sequential order.

Acknowledgment

Special thanks to Dr. Jerry J. Mallett for his help and encouragement.

Contents

12

How to Set Up Learning Centers • 57

How to Keep the Learning Center Orderly • 63

How to Maintain Learning Center Materials Daily • 64

How to Save Time in Setting Up Learning Centers • 64

Helpful Containers for Learning Center Materials • 64

4   SCIENCE LEARNING CENTER UNITS • 71

The Five Senses • 72

The Human Body • 106

1. Management

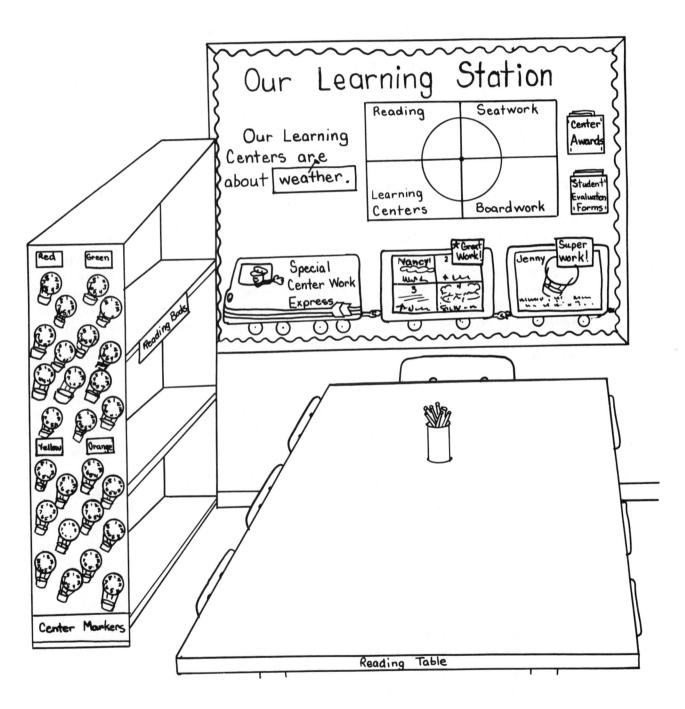

HOW TO MANAGE THE LEARNING CENTER SYSTEM

Teach the children in a traditional manner for the first three weeks of the school year. Assign morning seatwork to all of the children. Then work with small groups of children to assess their reading abilities.

Establish four reading groups based on ability and give each group a color name: red, yellow, orange, or green.

After the four groups have been established, introduce the children to a new morning routine. (See the sample Morning Schedule on page 18.) Move the children every half-hour to four areas of the classroom to do seatwork, boardwork, reading, and learning center activities (one child per learning center).

A Color Wheel (which is described later in this section) displayed near the reading area aids in the clockwise movement of the four groups to the four areas of the room.

Turn the Color Wheel clockwise after you have completed one half-hour with a reading group. Rotate the groups until each one has completed the four areas. (This takes approximately two hours every morning.) Thus, using the Color Wheel shown here, the orange group (five children) is at the reading table with you. The yellow group (seven children) is at the seatwork area. The red group (eight children) is working at the individual learning centers (numbers 1 through 8) around the edge of the room. The green group (six children) is at the boardwork area. The seatwork tables and boardwork tables can each accommodate two children.

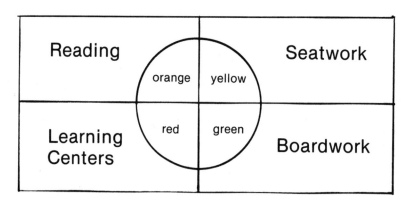

Have a makeup time of approximately 15 minutes after all four reading groups have finished so that children with incomplete work (which has been placed in a box labeled Makeup) can complete their work. The other children should use this time for games or books.

The afternoon schedule then consists of such whole-group activities as math, writing, gym, health, science, art, and social studies.

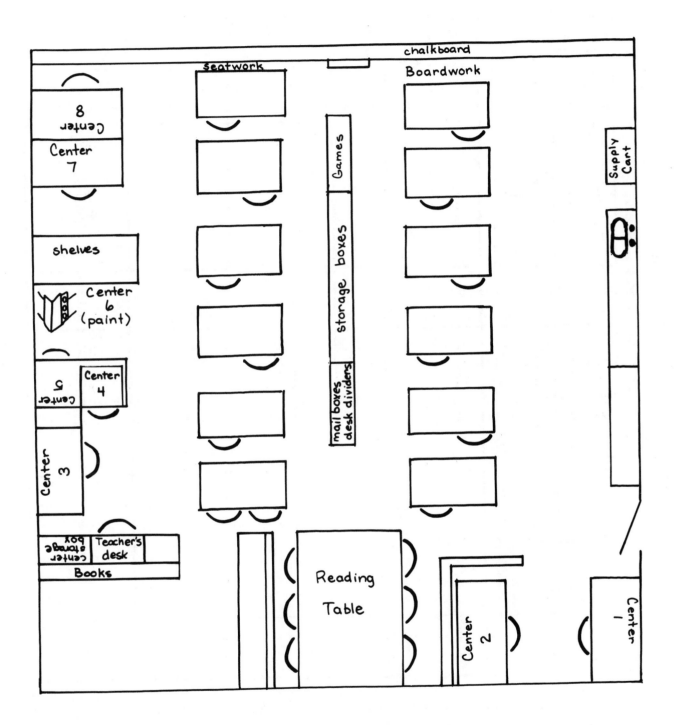

MORNING SCHEDULE

GROUP	8:30–9:00	9:00–9:30	9:30–10:00	10:00–10:15	10:15–10:45	10:45–11:15	11:15–11:30
Orange	Whole class is at seatwork and boardwork desks for opening and seatwork, boardwork directions.	Reading	Seatwork	Recess	Boardwork	Learning centers	Makeup
Yellow		Seatwork	Boardwork	Recess	Learning centers	Reading	Makeup
Red		Learning centers	Reading	Recess	Seatwork	Boardwork	Makeup
Green		Boardwork	Learning centers	Recess	Seatwork	Reading	Makeup

Rotation diagram (9:00–10:00):

Reading	Seatwork
orange	yellow
red	green
Learning Centers	Boardwork

Reading	Seatwork
red	orange
green	yellow
Learning Centers	Boardwork

Rotation diagram (10:15–11:15):

Reading	Seatwork
yellow	green
orange	red
Learning Centers	Boardwork

Reading	Seatwork
green	red
yellow	orange
Learning Centers	Boardwork

18

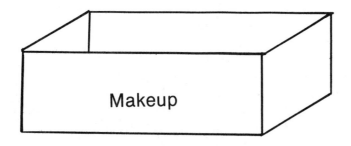

HOW TO MAKE A COLOR WHEEL

You need the following materials:

One piece of 14-by-22-inch blue posterboard

One circular piece of white posterboard 7 inches in diameter

One brass fastener ½ inch long

One black, red, yellow, orange, and green marking pen

One yardstick

Use the yardstick and the black marking pen to divide the blue posterboard into fourths. Write each of the four room areas (reading, seatwork, learning centers, and boardwork) in a different section of the posterboard. Use the yardstick and black marking pen again to divide the circular piece of posterboard into fourths. Color one-fourth of the circular piece red, one-fourth yellow, one-fourth green, and one-fourth orange. (The color arrangement depends on the order in which you want the four groups to move to the four areas.) Use the brass fastener to connect the center of the Color Wheel to the center of the blue posterboard.

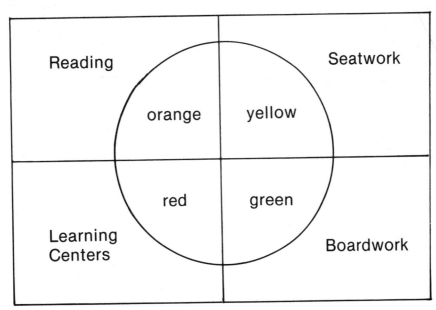

HOW TO KEEP TRACK OF EACH CHILD
AT THE LEARNING CENTERS

Reproduce a marker for each child.

(This book contains a center marker page in each Science Unit.) Sort the markers into the four color groups. Write the name of each child in the red group on an individual marker and circle a different number on each child's marker in the red group with a permanent marking pen. In this way each child in the red group starts at a different learning center.

Write the names and circle the numbers on the markers for the orange, yellow, and green groups in the same way.

Give the markers to each child to color and cut out. It is helpful to have each child color his or her own marker the color of his or her own group, especially with the first set of learning centers.

After the children have colored and cut out their markers, staple them onto a bulletin board or divider in the four groups. The markers should be near the reading area since the children move there after they finish the centers.

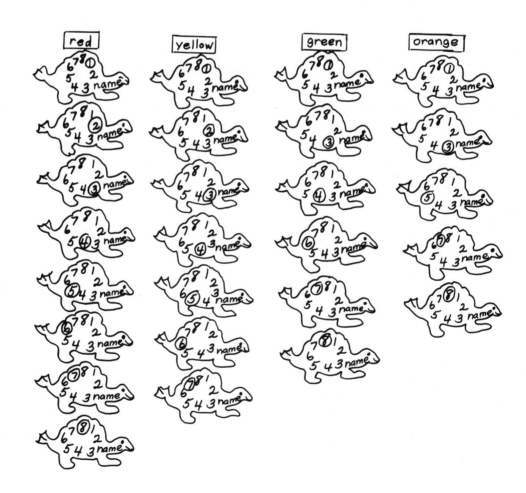

When the child has finished the learning center, he or she moves with the group to the reading area. The child finds his or her marker on the bulletin board or divider and, using a permanent marking pen, puts an "X" on the number of the learning center he or she has just finished. Then the child circles the next number in clockwise order, which is the number of the learning center where he or she will work the following day. The child continues this pattern daily until he or she has completed all learning centers (one per day). Thus, the child would do a total of eight learning centers, according to the dinosaur marker.

If a child is absent, mark "Ab" next to the number of that child's learning center. Then circle the following day's number. The learning centers missed due to absences are *not* made up. This is essential in keeping one child per learning center.

Tips for Numbering Markers in the Same Group

1. If you anticipate that two children within the same group will interact at the learning centers, do not number their markers consecutively. Put another child between them when you are assigning the numbers.

2. If a child, Bill for example, has difficulty following directions, start him at Learning Center 3 and have a more independent child, Diane, start at Learning Center 4. In this way, Diane will have completed Learning Center 3 the previous day and can help Bill with directions. Thus, Bill does not have to interrupt you for help.

HOW TO EVALUATE THE LEARNING CENTERS

When the Color Wheel is rotated, the children move from the learning centers to the reading area. They should bring the work they did at the centers to you so that the two of you can make a joint decision regarding a grade. Shown here are three possible evaluation forms that can be used. The first, Evaluation for _____ Learning Centers, is completed by you for the entire class. The second, Self-Evaluation Sheet, can be stapled to each child's learning center work and filled in by the child. The third, Learning Center Evaluation, is completed by you and can be attached to each child's regular grade card.

EVALUATION FOR _____ LEARNING CENTERS

Child's Name	Center 1	Center 2	Center 3	Center 4	Center 5	Center 6	Center 7	Center 8
Green group								
Yellow group								
Red group								
Orange group								

SELF-EVALUATION SHEET

Name _____   Date _____

Today I worked at Learning Center _____.
My learning center work was

Today I worked at Learning Center _____.
My learning center work was

Today I worked at Learning Center _____.
My learning center work was

Today I worked at Learning Center _____.
My learning center work was

Today I worked at Learning Center _____.
My learning center work was

23

LEARNING CENTER EVALUATION

Name _____   Date _____

	Very Good	Satisfactory	Needs to Improve
1. Works independently			
2. Understands directions			
3. Makes effective use of learning center time			
4. Helps other children with directions			
5. Takes care of learning center materials			

6. Additional comments: _____

_____

_____

_____

_____

_____

_____

_____

_____

_____

_____

_____

_____

                                    _____
                                         Teacher's signature

HOW TO RECRUIT PARENTS' HELP

Parents can be a very important part of your learning center program. Send a letter to parents the first day of school to request their help. (See the following letter.) You might make copies of the letter on colored paper and remind the students to return the blue (or whatever color) letter.

As soon as you have received all of the completed I Need Your Help letters, use the Parent Help form to compile all your data. Here is a sample of a completed form.

People who can help	Phone no.	Field Trips	Parties	Laminate	Type	Home Help	School Help
1. Mr. Brown	555-1234	x		x			x
2. Mrs. Doe	555-4230		x		x	x	
3. Ms. Green	555-4010	x		x		x	x
4. Mrs. High	555-3030		x	x			x
5. Mr. Ice	555-4012	x		x			x
6. Mrs. Jones	555-8032		x		x	x	x
7. Ms. Land	555-9040	x		x			x
8. Mr. Muncy	555-4011		x		x		
9. Mrs. Pool	555-3144	x			x	x	x

People who can help at school
A = every week; B = every other week; C = once a month

Name	Mon. A.M.	Mon. P.M.	Tues. A.M.	Tues. P.M.	Wed. A.M.	Wed. P.M.	Thurs. A.M.	Thurs. P.M.	Fri. A.M.	Fri. P.M.
Mr. Brown		A				A				
Mrs. Doe	B				B				B	
Ms. Green			A					A		
Mrs. High				C				C		C
Mr. Ice	A				A					
Mrs. Jones				A				A		
Ms. Land	B				B				B	
Mr. Muncy			A					A		
Mrs. Pool		B				B				

I NEED YOUR HELP

Date _____

Dear Parent:

Please fill out the following and return within seven days:

Child's name: _____

Parent's name: _____ Phone No. _____

Pets: (kind and name) _____

Child's favorite activities or special interests: _____

_____

Please print the name that you wish to have your child learn to write:

first: _____ last: _____

Would you be interested in helping on walking field trips? _____

Would you be interested in helping with parties? _____

Would you be willing to laminate or type materials? _____

Would you be able to prepare materials sent to your home? _____

Would you like to help in our room on a regular schedule with small groups of children or preparing materials? _____

  If your answer is yes, how often could you help? Check one:

Every week _____ Every other week _____ Once a month _____

What days do you prefer? _____ A.M. _____ P.M. _____

I would appreciate any information you feel would be beneficial to me in helping your child. (Please use the back of this paper.) Thank you very much for taking the time to fill out this sheet. It is helpful to me throughout the year.

Sincerely,

_____

Your child's teacher

PARENT HELP FORM

People who can help	Phone no.									

People who can help at school
A = every week; B = every other week; C = once a month

Name	Mon. A.M.	Mon. P.M.	Tues. A.M.	Tues. P.M.	Wed. A.M.	Wed. P.M.	Thurs. A.M.	Thurs. P.M.	Fri. A.M.	Fri. P.M.

Naturally, this initial request for help will probably not be the only one you will make to parents. During the school year you may need additional assistance. Keep a supply of Parent Help Notes handy for those times during the year when you need to contact parents for help. (See pages 29 and 30.)

HOW TO EXPLAIN LEARNING CENTERS TO PARENTS

To familiarize parents with the learning center system, send home a letter on the first day of school explaining that the centers will be beginning in about the third week of September. Since many parents work and are unable to visit the school during the day, an evening meeting should be arranged to discuss the centers with parents. Do this after you have begun using learning centers, usually some time in October. (See pages 31–33.)

HOW TO EXPLAIN LEARNING CENTERS TO A SUBSTITUTE TEACHER

The learning center program should not be interrupted because of your absence. To avoid any problems during an absence, make a copy of the Substitute Teacher Information form and keep it in your plan book, substitute teacher folder, or wherever the substitute's materials are placed. You might also want to include a floor plan. (See pages 34 and 35.)

PARENT HELP NOTES

Date _____

Dear Parent,

I would appreciate having the following people come to our room at the times I have scheduled.

If you *cannot* come, please contact me by _____.
date

Thank you very much.

Sincerely,

_____
Your child's teacher

Date	Monday	Tuesday	Wednesday	Thursday	Friday
A.M.	Name	Name	Name	Name	Name
P.M.	Name	Name	Name	Name	Name

Date _____

Dear _____,

Would you be willing to help in our room on _____ ?
                                             date   time

Please circle Yes or No and return the note tomorrow.

Thank you very much.

Sincerely,

_____
Your child's teacher

Date _____

Dear _____,

I will need help with _____.

Please circle one time that would be convenient for you:

_____
date   time

_____
date   time

_____
date   time

Please return the note tomorrow.

Thank you very much.

Sincerely,

_____
Your child's teacher

LETTER OF EXPLANATION

September _____

Dear Parent,

During the first few weeks of school I have been reviewing the skills your child has learned in the past. The children have been given a variety of tests. I wanted to find out where each child was regarding these skills and take him or her from that point on.

Today we began a new morning routine that we will follow all year. The children have been divided into four groups based on reading ability. The four groups are red, green, yellow, and orange. The children move every half-hour to each of four areas of the classroom to do seatwork, boardwork, reading, and learning center activities.

A Color Wheel, shown below, helps all of us to keep track of where we are working.

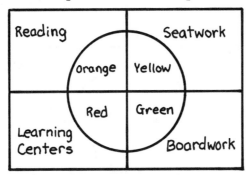

In this diagram the orange group is working with me at the reading area, the yellow group is doing seatwork (math and phonics papers), the green group is at the boardwork area (copying some type of work from the chalkboard), and the red group is working at eight different learning centers (one child per learning center). At the end of half an hour, the Color Wheel is turned clockwise and all of the groups move to the next area. The groups continue to move this way until each group has completed all four areas.

A makeup time is given after the children have completed all four areas. This enables all of the children to finish their morning work. In the afternoon we have whole-group activities: math, science, art, social studies, handwriting, and so on.

Participation in learning centers will be a new experience to many of our children. I have prepared activities for eight individual learning centers covering the following skills: math, art, social studies, science, reading, listening, handwriting, and coordination.

There are several reasons I am teaching with learning centers: (1) The classroom is quieter; (2) a structured routine is followed daily; (3) the children learn to follow directions; (4) independent study habits are established; (5) the children can pace themselves to work for 30 minutes; (6) the children learn to evaluate themselves; and (7) a wide variety of subjects provide experiences in learning something new, reinforcing old skills, or developing creativity.

During the next eight school days the learning centers will be based on the theme _____ _____. If you have books, records, or games about this learning center topic, please send them. You are welcome to visit us any morning to see our learning centers in action. I am looking forward to meeting you.

The beginning weeks of learning centers may present many new adjustments. We will have a routine established within a week. Thank you for your support.

Since I want to be sure that this letter arrived at your house, please sign and return the happy face to me tomorrow. Thank you.

Sincerely,

_____
Your child's teacher

Name _____

Are you planning to come for a brief
visit to see our learning centers?
___ Yes ___ No

LEARNING CENTERS' EVENING MEETING

October _____

Dear Parent,

Since many people are unable to visit the classroom during the school day, I would like to invite you and your child to a group meeting. The meeting will be held in Room _____ at the

_____ School on _____

at _____ P.M. It will last approximately one hour.

The meeting will consist of the following:

1. A brief presentation of the learning centers approach that we are using daily in our classroom.
2. A question-and-answer period.
3. An opportunity for you and your child to visit our room to see learning centers.

I appreciate the support that you have given me this year. I would like to know how many people plan to attend the meeting. Please return the following note by _____.

Sincerely,

_____
Your child's teacher

------------------------------- cut along line -------------------------------

_____
Your child's name

Please check one of the following:

_____ We will be able to attend the meeting on _____.
The number planning to attend is _____.

_____ We will not be able to attend the meeting.

_____
Parent's signature

SUBSTITUTE TEACHER INFORMATION

Please see _____ in Room _____ if you have questions.

teacher

When the children arrive at _____ they sit at desks located at the _____

time

areas of the room. They will remain at these desks for the opening activities and seatwork and boardwork directions.

The children can do the following activities before school begins at _____ : _____

_____ .

Follow the lesson plans in my plan book on _____ .

Seatwork and boardwork papers are in _____ .

Reading books and manuals are _____ .

Special information: _____

_____

After you have finished the opening activities and the seatwork and boardwork directions the children are ready to begin their morning work in four different groups. The children are divided into four groups based on reading ability: red, yellow, orange, and green. All groups are listed

on individual markers on _____ .

Key students who can help you are: _____(red group), _____

(yellow group), _____ (orange group), and _____

(green group).

The classroom is divided into four areas: seatwork, boardwork, reading, and learning centers

(_____ are set up around the room). Extra materials for the learning centers are in a

no.

_____ located _____ .

A master list of the learning centers is located _____ .

When you are ready to begin reading, go to the Color Wheel on the _____ .

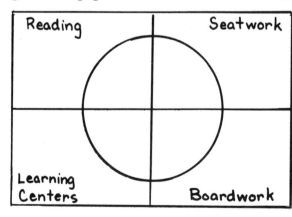

One group will go to the seatwork side of the room and begin seatwork.
One group will go to the boardwork side of the room and begin boardwork.

One group will look at its own markers on _____, then each child in that group
will go to an individual learning center. (Only one child will be in a learning center at a time.)
One group will go to the reading table with you to begin reading.

After 30 minutes, say, "_____" (this is our signal for quieting the whole room).
Turn the Color Wheel clockwise. All four groups move clockwise to seatwork, boardwork, learning centers, and reading.

Use the makeup box on _____ for work that is unfinished when it is time to change areas.

The children who come to the reading table will use a permanent marking pen (in _____)
to X out today's completed number on their marker. Then they will circle their next learning
center number, going clockwise on the marker.
Check the learning center work at the reading table before you begin the reading group. Record

the grade on the Evaluation for _____ Learning Centers form in

_____ .

The graded work will go into the children's mailboxes or Go Home box until it is sent home at
dismissal time.
After all four reading groups are finished (approximately two hours), allow a makeup time (approximately 15 minutes). The children who have work in the makeup box take their work to the
seatwork, boardwork, or learning centers areas to finish. The rest of the children who have all

of their morning work completed may _____

_____ .

When the makeup time is completed, all of the children return to the desks at the _____

_____ areas of the room.
Continue to follow my lesson plans for the remaining activities of the day.

Additional information: _____

_____

_____

_____

_____

_____

_____

_____

_____

_____

QUESTIONS YOU MAY HAVE ABOUT MANAGEMENT

How many learning centers do I need to set up?

You will need as many learning centers as the total number of children in your largest reading group.

How often do I change a set of learning centers?

If you have eight learning centers, you will change them at the end of an eight-day period. Each child will have completed eight learning centers.

Do I have days when I do not have learning centers set up?

There will occasionally be one or two "come up for air" days before a new set of learning centers is set up.

How do I manage the four groups on those days?

The groups continue to rotate with the Color Wheel order. During the learning center time block, they go to an empty learning center to do an activity—a special art project, a task card activity, a picture dictionary assignment, and so on.

What do I use for seatwork and boardwork?

Phonics, math, reading dittos, or individualized reading assignments given at the reading group can be used for seatwork. Boardwork consists of copying some type of work from the chalkboard. Often the work is correlated with the learning center theme. Other boardwork activities are spelling, creative writing, daily journals, and dictionary assignments.

How can I use this system if I have more than four reading ability groups?

Try these suggestions to help you keep four groups:
1. Send a few children to another teacher for reading only.
2. Combine a few children from one class with a few of your students (perhaps you could teach this group for one semester and the other teacher for the other semester).

What can I do with a child whose reading ability changes?

The child can be moved to another group prior to the first day of a new set of learning centers.

How can I use the Color Wheel to meet the needs of children who must leave my class for special instruction?

You can control the order of the groups on the Color Wheel. It is preferable for students to leave during their seatwork or boardwork time blocks. The work from these two areas can be completed during makeup time.

How can I vary this management system to meet my needs?

Try these suggestions:

1. If you switch students for reading instruction, you could group them according to math ability.

2. You could have four groups of children going to five learning centers (two children per learning center in each group). You could accommodate 10 students in a reading group. Learning centers would then be changed at the end of five days.

3. You may prefer to have five groups moving to five room areas for reading, phonics (reading workbooks), math, boardwork, and learning centers. The activities would last 30 minutes.

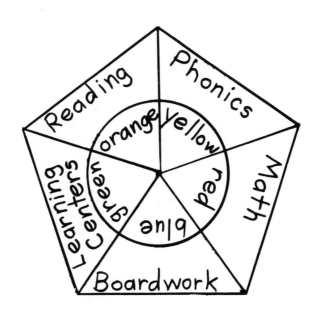

2. Room Environment

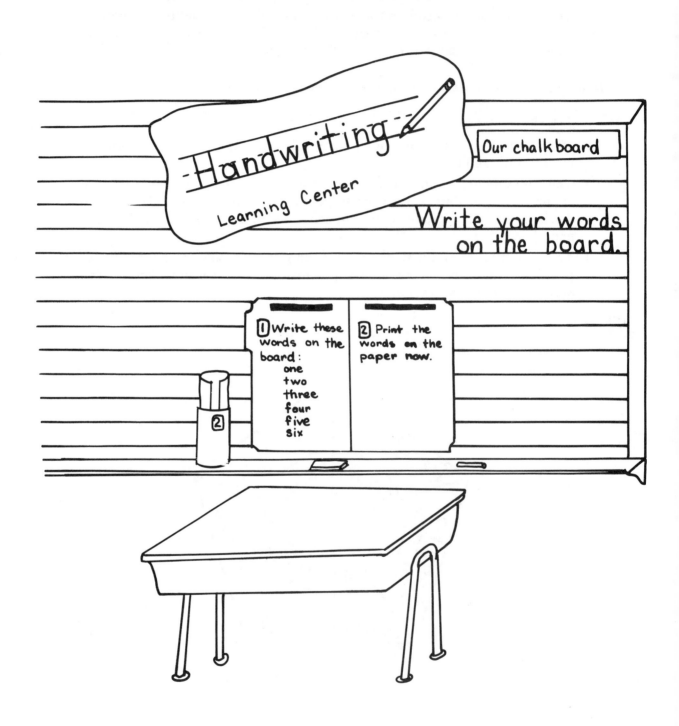

Handwriting
Learning Center

Our chalkboard

Write your words
on the board.

1 Write these words on the board:
one
two
three
four
five
six

2 Print the words on the paper now.

HOW TO SET UP THE CLASSROOM IN FOUR AREAS

The arrangement of the furniture in the classroom is important in creating a good learning environment. The room should be set up to give the students the freedom to move physically and academically from one area to another.

Prior to the first day of school arrange the furniture to create four areas: seatwork, boardwork, reading, and learning centers, even though you may not be starting the four-group Color Wheel movement pattern for three or four weeks. It is easier to develop a set routine in the beginning weeks of the school year than to rearrange the classroom when you start the four-group movement.

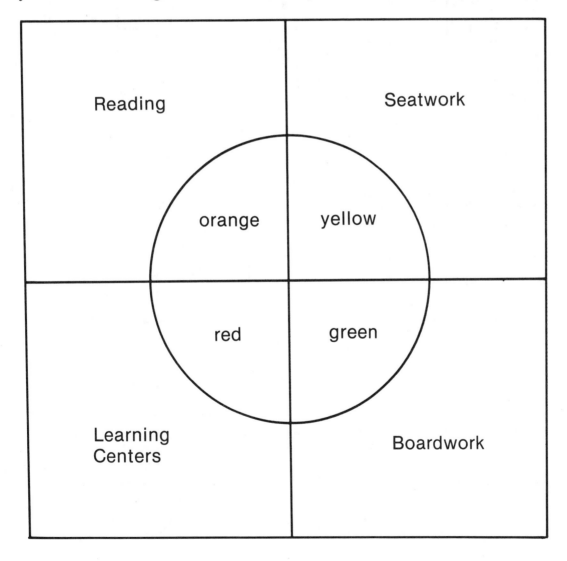

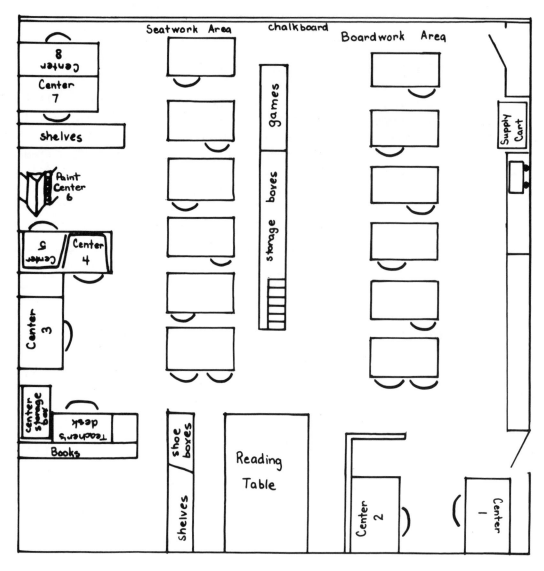

Floor Plan A

The main area of the classroom should be divided into two parts, for seat-work and boardwork. Bookcases or storage boxes can be placed in a long row to serve as a divider between the seatwork and boardwork areas. Desks (one for each child) can be arranged on either side of the main divider in the seatwork and boardwork areas. The desks in the boardwork area will usually face a chalkboard (since the children will be copying assignments from the chalkboard). In the seat-work area, the desks do not have to face the chalkboard. The seatwork activities are mainly ditto sheets and workbook assignments. (See Floor Plan A.)

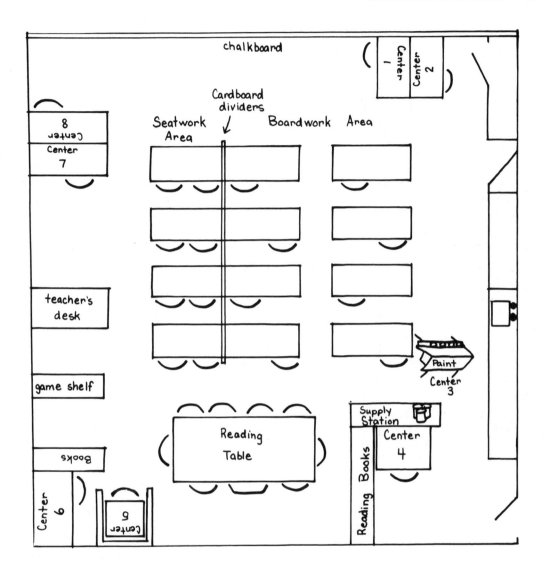

Floor Plan B

Cardboard can be used as an effective divider if bookcases are unavailable. Several thin 3½-foot-square pieces can be placed between a row of seatwork desks and a row of boardwork desks. When the children are seated they cannot see over the top of the cardboard. This eliminates interaction between the two groups. (If you have taller children you may want higher pieces of cardboard.) The cardboard pieces can easily be removed for whole-group activities, such as parties, cooking, and art projects. (See Floor Plan B.)

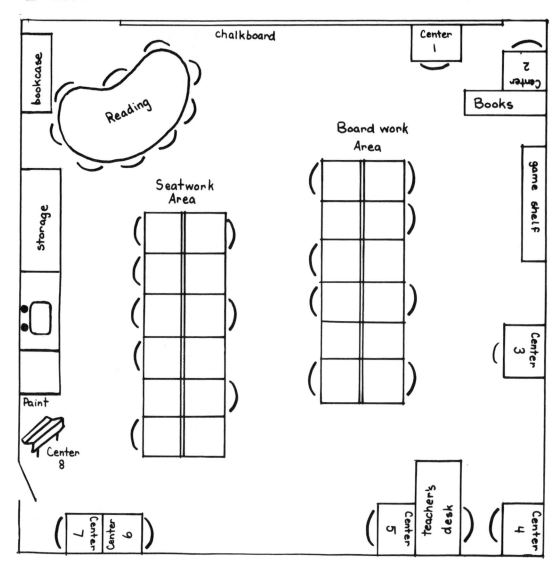

Floor Plan C

If your floor space is limited, you can line up a row of boardwork desks side by side. The desk legs can be wired together to form a permanent row. Make a similar row of an equal number of boardwork desks. Place the two rows of desks so they face each other. Leave just enough space between the two rows to stand 3½-foot-square pieces of cardboard so that when the children are seated, the cardboard is above their eye level, thus preventing interaction between the two groups. Two rows of seatwork desks can be arranged in a similar way. Desk dividers can be used to separate the children within the seatwork and boardwork groups. (See Floor Plan C.)

HOW TO MAKE A DESK DIVIDER

Materials needed:

Three pieces of 16-by-18-inch cardboard
Two yards of 3-inch wide duct tape or Con-Tact paper strips
Four yards of 18-inch wide Con-Tact paper (woodgrain or solid color)
Scissors

Procedure:

1. Lay the three pieces of cardboard on the floor or table about ½ inch apart. Wrap the duct tape or Con-Tact paper strips around the edges of the cardboard pieces A and B and C and D (see the illustration). The duct tape acts as a hinge while joining all three cardboard pieces to make the divider.

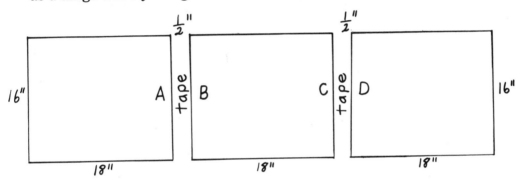

2. Lay the divider flat on the floor or table. Cover both the front and back sides of the divider with Con-Tact paper.

3. For easy handling and storage, fold piece A over BC and piece D over A.

How to use:

The desk divider can be used effectively on an individual child's desk to block out any classroom distractions. (Children frequently choose to put a divider on their own desk because they know when they need one.) The desk divider is an ideal way to create two separate quiet, independent work areas on a desk or table that seats two children. It is especially helpful to use the desk dividers during the seatwork period of the day.

Two desk dividers can be placed on a table to create space for two separate learning centers. (See illustration A, page 44.)

Desk dividers can also be placed on the reading table to separate children working independently on tests or workbook pages, as shown in illustration B, page 44.

You might also place a desk divider on a learning center table. The direction file folder, material envelopes, pictures, and the like can be attached to the divider with clothespins. (See illustration C, page 44.)

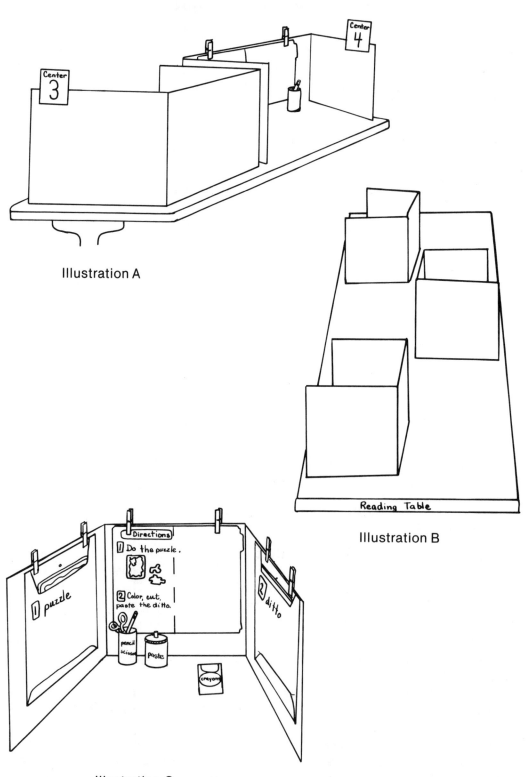

Illustration A

Illustration B

Illustration C

How to store:

An effective storage container can be made by cutting off the top of a large cardboard box and standing it on one side. Put the storage box in an area that will be easily accessible to the children, since they will be responsible for handling the dividers. The illustration here shows how the dividers can be stored on a bookcase.

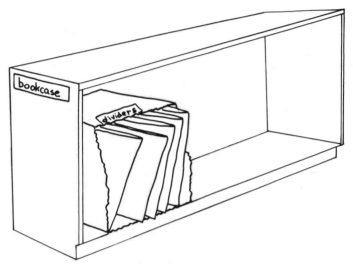

How to arrange the reading area:

The location of the reading area is of primary importance. In order to maintain good classroom control, you should be able to see or hear all of the children from your position in the reading area, so it may be preferable to place the reading area behind the seatwork and boardwork areas. A portable chalkboard, chart racks, and other teaching aids can be utilized in the reading area.

A bulletin board, a portable screen or divider, or a bookcase (with a solid back) are desirable to have near the reading area. One of these needs to be easily accessible to the children and you. The Color Wheel will be located there, and individual children's markers will be stapled or tacked to the bulletin board, bookcase, or screen or divider. (See the illustration on page 46.)

How to assign desks:

Another important factor to consider in room arrangement is the assignment of desks. Each child can have a permanently assigned desk to use before school and during the whole-group activities of the day. In order to accommodate the mobility of the four groups to seatwork, boardwork, learning centers, and reading, all of the desk tops can be shared by everyone. (You may need to establish a rule that everyone works on desk tops only.)

Supplies such as pencils, crayons, scissors, and paste can be kept at a central location (countertop, three-tiered cart, or bookcase, for example). The children can use these supplies during seatwork, boardwork, and learning centers.

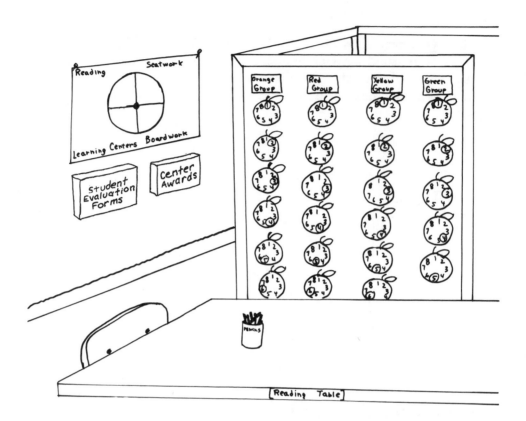

You may want each child to have a small box of supplies in his or her own desk so that the child can carry the box to the various work areas of the room.

There is an alternative method for seating that allows for maximum mobility in the classroom. The children do not have any assigned desks; only the tops of the desks are used, not the insides. (You may prefer to turn the desks so the open ends are away from the seated children.)

Each child needs a shoe box or something similar for his or her supplies. The shoe boxes are stored on a bookshelf that is easily accessible to the children. When a child enters the room each morning, he or she puts the shoe box on an empty seatwork or boardwork desk. The child uses this desk before school and during whole-group activities. When the child moves with his or her group to learning centers, seatwork, boardwork, and reading, he or she brings the shoe box. During reading, the shoe box is put on the bookshelf.

If you obtain a shoe box for each child during the summer (most shoe stores have extra boxes), you can tape a tagboard name card to the lid and cover it with clear Con-Tact paper before the first day of school.

Here are some tips for using the shoe boxes (after the four groups have been established):

1. Put a 1-inch red construction-paper square on the top of the lid with masking tape (or use a red sticker) for children in the red group.

2. Put a 2-inch clear Con-tact paper square over the red square. (This helps to prevent the child from picking off the red square.)

3. Put the appropriate color squares on the boxes of the other three groups. (See the illustration.)

The color coding is especially meaningful during the first week you use the four areas of the room. The colored square is a good visual aid to help the child remember his or her group, enabling him or her to move independently to the four areas. It is also helpful all year for a substitute teacher.

HOW TO FIND FURNITURE FOR LEARNING CENTERS

After you have established the seatwork, boardwork, and reading areas, tentatively decide on the number of learning centers you want to use and figure out the location of each one. Remember that children are not fussy about where they work. They enjoy the freedom of being in unconventional places.

The learning center areas can be used by the children for games, books, or science tables during the initial weeks of school prior to the four-group Color Wheel movement pattern.

You will probably have to scrounge for furniture from a variety of sources for the learning centers. Here are some suggestions:

1. Ask your maintenance person about extra pieces of furniture in the building.

2. Trade furniture with other teachers in your building.

3. Go to garage sales for inexpensive furniture.

4. Post a notice listing the kinds of furniture you want in the hall or your room in the opening days of school.

5. Send a letter (see the sample) to the parents of your children in September requesting unwanted furniture or asking to borrow furniture for the school year.

WE NEED FURNITURE!

Date _____

Dear Parent:

We need your help. We are in the process of developing learning centers in our classroom that we will use all year. Perhaps you have a few items that are no longer of use to you but would be helpful for us. Please check any items that you could donate and return this list within two days. The items will be used by all of the children. They will not be returned, unless special arrangements are indicated.

Thank you for your cooperation.

Sincerely,

_____
Your child's teacher

_____ bookcases

_____ rugs

_____ 2-by-4-foot boards

_____ soft drink bottle cases

_____ couch or loveseat

_____ rocking chair

_____ child's table

_____ telephone table

_____ refrigerator-size box

_____ 18-inch or larger cardboard

      squares

_____ burlap or drapes

_____ other _____

_____ window shades

_____ wire

_____ clothespins

_____ coffee cans (1-, 2-, or 3-pound)

_____ margarine tubs with lids

_____ orange juice cans

_____ soup cans

_____ milk cartons (half gallon)

_____ trays

_____ pitchers (pint-size, plastic)

_____ dishpans

_____ snack trays

_____

_____

_____

_____

Signed _____ Phone no. _____

HOW TO CREATE LEARNING CENTER AREAS

Here are several suggestions for creating your learning centers:

1. An easel can be used for painting or for an Art Learning Center.

2. Use masking tape on the floor to create a learning center boundary. The child can sit on a carpet sample inside the taped area with the learning center materials.

3. An area rug or piece of carpeting (approximately 3 by 6 feet) makes an effective space for a learning center.

4. Use a countertop area for a learning center (a messy activity can be placed there).

5. Make a portable learning center by using clothespins to hang directions and materials from a desk divider. This learning center can be stored on top of a counter or bookcase. The child can move the desk divider to an empty seat-work or boardwork desk during his or her learning center time block.

6. A large refrigerator box can be placed on the floor upside down. A door and windows may be cut out of the box to make an excellent Listening Learning Center.

7. A section of the chalkboard can be used for the Handwriting Learning Center. Directions can be written on the board or on a file folder (easily attached to the chalkboard with magnets).

8. A telephone table with the seat attached makes a good learning center. It has a good surface for writing and a cubbyhole for materials.

9. A bulletin board area is another place to create a learning center. It is a great space for matching manipulative activities.

10. Balance a board (approximately 2 by 4 feet) on two file cabinets (two-drawer size) or on two equal stacks of soft drink bottle cases. This unit works well set up against a wall.

11. A file cabinet or any metal surface can be used for a manipulative games area. Pieces of magnetic tape can be attached to the backs of cut-out pieces in order to stick to the metal surface.

12. Hang curtains, plastic sheets, burlap, or cardboard on wires suspended from the ceiling. These can serve as lightweight dividers. Direction folders can be stapled or clothespinned to them.

13. Window shades that are permanently mounted above windows can also be used. Direction folders or pictures can be clothespinned to them.

14. A clothesline can be strung across the room. Direction file folders or pictures can then be pinned to it.

15. A fishnet can also be used to display materials.

3. Organizing the Learning Centers

50

The purpose of this learning center section is to present general ideas for creating, developing, and managing learning center activities for a variety of subjects.

Suggestions are given in detail to encourage educators who are planning to use learning center activities for the first time.

In addition, we have given several shortcuts and techniques which we hope will be helpful for experienced learning center educators.

HOW TO DEVELOP LEARNING CENTERS

1. Decide on the number of learning centers you want to use in your classroom. The number of learning centers must equal the number of children in your largest reading group. With this arrangement there will be no more than one child working in each learning center.

2. Choose a theme that is appealing to your children: a cartoon character, animals, senses, a season, a holiday, or famous people, for example.

3. Sort through any commercial or teacher-made theme materials to which you have access: pictures, bulletin board sets, books, puzzles, manipulative materials, sewing cards, flashcards, magnetic board sets, flannelboard sets, learning games, pocket charts, tape cassettes, records, filmstrips, science kits, transparencies, children's weekly magazines or newspapers, old workbooks, old textbooks, and sets of spirit duplicating masters. (A commercial coloring book or a set of spirit duplicating masters is a great asset in the development of learning centers. They can be used for seatwork and boardwork ideas in addition to the specific learning centers.)

4. Keep all of the theme materials together in a large storage box. An ideal box has a lid and is 24 by 16 by 12 inches high. (Most discount stores sell these boxes in flat packages.)

5. Correlate the accumulated theme materials with the skills you want to introduce, develop, or reinforce in various areas. A set of learning centers should encompass several disciplines, such as math, reading, science, social studies, handwriting, listening, art, and coordination.

6. Determine the length of the learning center period. A half-hour time block works well with most elementary-school children.

7. Prepare a variety of learning center activities that are manipulative, written, self-checking, visual, auditory, and tactile.

8. Develop the following boardwork activities:

Boardwork Activities

Fact Cards

Prepare facts about the learning center theme on numbered index cards that can be referred to in the lesson plans by card number. Write a few sentence facts on the chalkboard for the student to copy and illustrate.

Theme Riddles

Prepare the riddles in the same manner as the fact cards, or write a different riddle on the chalkboard. (See the illustrations.) Students may share their riddles with the class at a prearranged time that day.

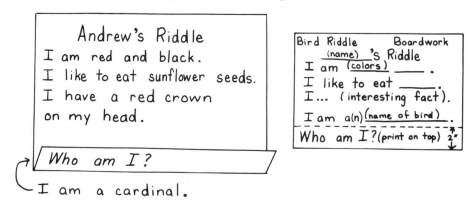

Poems

Poems may also be written on index cards for easy teacher reference. Students copy poems from the chalkboard and illustrate them. Students may also write their own poems.

Picture-Word Reference Charts

Put four or eight words and pictures on each posterboard chart (see the illustration). Students may copy the words and illustrate them for one assignment. On another day they may write a few sentences using the chart as a reference in expressing their ideas.

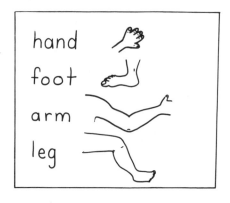

Word Bank Charts

Use large lined chart paper. Discuss the theme with the students. Together develop a vocabulary that you will write on the chart. Students use the word bank chart as a reference for creative writing.

Dictionary-Pictionary Idea

Use eight copies of the same reference book. Make assignments pertaining to the book's theme. For example, find four animals that live on a farm. Write two sentences describing them.

Class Shape Books

Provide posterboard patterns of a theme object. Students trace the patterns on handwriting paper and cut them out. Students then write a creative story about the objects and color in the outlines. Combine all of the students' stories into a class shape book with a matching cover, such as the one shown here of a class dinosaur book.

Puppets

Each student can make a puppet and write a story about it. For example:

My puppet's name is _____. She likes to _____. The illustrations here show a variety of puppets that can be made.

Journals

Make a journal for each student by folding several sheets of paper in half. Staple the sheets inside a folded piece of 9-by-12-inch construction paper. The student writes and perhaps illustrates a daily event.

Story Starters

Prepare several laminated tagboard strips or index cards with theme story starters written on them. (An example is shown in the illustration.) Students copy the story starter on paper, write an ending, and illustrate it.

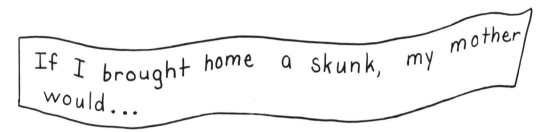

Miscellaneous Boardwork Activities

Number words, spelling words, rhyming words, contractions, and math problems are examples of activities that you can write on the chalkboard in a variety of formats. (The illustration here shows one example.)

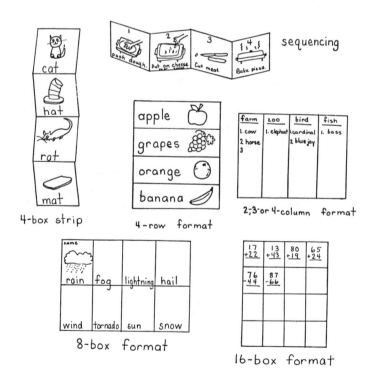

How to Save Time When Developing Learning Centers

1. Work with another teacher. It is extremely helpful if you can share materials and ideas with a teacher of the same grade level.

   a. You might begin by developing an identical set of learning centers based on one theme. Each person could be responsible for four different learning centers, including duplicate sets of directions and materials.

   b. Ideally each teacher could develop one complete set of eight different learning centers. Schedule the two sets of learning centers to begin on the same day. At the end of eight days, exchange the two sets of learning centers.

   c. By sharing, you create more time to plan additional sets of learning centers because you prepare only half of the sets of learning centers needed for a school year. You have someone with whom you can brainstorm ideas, seek encouragement, and share the many rewards.

2. Plan proper storage to keep all of your materials for one set of learning centers together so they can be reused. Get a large enough storage box that can be easily carried and stacked on top of similar boxes to save floor space. Label the boxes.

3. Make a master list of each set of learning centers.

   a. Indicate the learning center numbers, skill areas, and special materials needed for individual centers (books, audiovisual aids, and so on.)

   b. Attach the list to the inside of the storage box lid for easy accessibility at setup time. It reduces preparation time when you reuse the learning centers another year, and is a convenient reference for a substitute teacher.

   c. Keep a duplicate master list for each set of learning centers in one file folder. The lists are valuable for scheduling, preparing materials, ordering audiovisual aids, and planning for another year.

4. Construct durable learning centers for reuse.

   a. Laminate materials.

   b. Cut big posters in half prior to laminating so they will fit in the storage box.

   c. Use small margarine bowls with lids to keep small parts and gameboard pieces organized.

5. Recruit parents or student aides to help with laminating, running dittos, cutting paper, changing bulletin boards, setting up paint, and so on.

6. Label one storage box Learning Center Ideas and keep it in a convenient place. Put in it any materials you find that might be used for future learning centers. Jot down any good ideas: records, tape cassettes, books, or advertisements that may have learning center possibilities. Include snapshots of

learning centers, gameboards, and bulletin boards that you take at workshops or other classrooms. These ideas will be helpful when you find time to construct new learning centers.

Tips for Developing Your Initial Set of Learning Centers

1. Plan easy activities that reinforce previously taught skills. You may not be able to think of an activity for each discipline area, so you might have two Art Learning Centers or two Reading Learning Centers. The main thing is to plunge in and begin with easy ideas. Eventually, as you become more accustomed to developing learning centers, you can strive toward a variety of discipline areas and begin to think in terms of creating a particular learning center based on a new theme. (The discipline areas are natural guidelines to follow.)

2. Develop one main activity for each learning center.

3. Keep the directions very simple, enabling each child to complete the main activity independently. It is important that the child achieve success in completing the activity so that he or she will gain self-confidence in using learning centers. (This may be the first independent experience for many children.)

4. A book, puzzle, game, sewing card, or ditto sheet can be placed at each learning center as a secondary activity. These supplemental materials provide the faster child with more activities for the remainder of his or her learning center time. (You may prefer to have only one main activity at each learning center on the first day. You can then add supplemental materials that the children can complete rapidly. This allows you flexibility in the placement of materials.)

5. Determine other things (games or books from specific areas in the room) that may be used at the learning center if a child has time remaining. It is important that the child stay at the learning center for his or her entire time block. This keeps group interaction to a minimum.

How to Introduce a New Set of Learning Centers to the Class

1. Seat all of the children on the floor near the first learning center. (After you have finished the directions for the first learning center, the group continues to move with you to each additional center. It may take 30 to 45 minutes to explain eight learning centers. No additional directions will be necessary for the eight-day period.)

2. Explain the directions in consecutive order at each learning center.

3. Demonstrate any special equipment at the learning center.

4. Discuss the proper care of materials. If materials have been borrowed from the media center, you may want to emphasize special handling.

5. Indicate any activities that need to be checked by you before the child leaves the learning center. Work out a signal for the child so you don't forget to check his or her work.

6. Discuss cleanup rules. If the learning center is disorderly when a child goes to it, he or she should get the preceding child to clean up.

7. Allow time for questions at each learning center. By explaining a set of centers thoroughly, you will eliminate daily interruptions. A child may quietly ask another person in his or her group for additional help with directions.

HOW TO SET UP LEARNING CENTERS

The Listening Learning Center

Set up a tape recorder on a table or the floor inside a large refrigerator box that has been turned upside down with a door cut out.

1. Put this learning center near an electrical outlet (batteries are not practical, especially if you are paying for them).

2. Place the center near the reading table where it will be easily accessible to you if help is needed.

3. Do not use a headset; just keep the volume low. (Headsets often become unplugged and complicate independent usage.) Most tapes are approximately 10 to 15 minutes in length, so the low noise level is not distracting to the other students.

4. Use a marking pen to number the buttons on the tape recorder: 1 (go), 2 (stop), and 3 (rewind). Put an X on any remaining buttons. You may prefer to color code the three buttons with different colors of tape. (See the illustration.) Masking tape colored with marking pens works well too. You might also place a matching chart near the tape recorder as a visual aid.

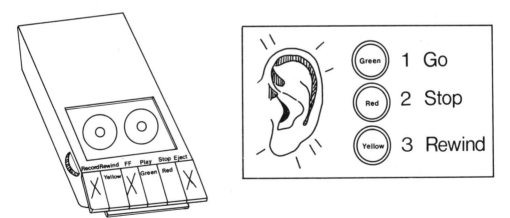

The child can then easily operate the tape recorder by pushing the buttons in order.

Listening Center Ideas

1. Use a commercial story cassette tape and book. Make a puppet.
2. Listen to a teacher-taped storybook. Draw a picture about the best part.
3. Listen to a teacher-taped story starter, then write a few sentences about it.
4. Do a science experiment by following teacher-taped recorded directions.
5. Operate a filmstrip previewer by following teacher-taped directions.
6. Make up a story and record it on a tape. Illustrate the story.
7. Do a worksheet and then listen to a tape with the answers.
8. Take short dictation from a tape of any subject area. Check the dictation with an answer key.

The Painting Learning Center

Set up an easel.

1. Cover the easel and tray with newspaper.
2. Put five baby food jars half full of tempera paint and brushes in the tray.
3. Hang an adult's short-sleeved shirt on the easel.
4. Clothespin 18-by-24-inch paper to the back of the easel. (Pin up four sheets daily. Each child will take one sheet and pin it to the front of the easel when it is his or her turn to paint.)

If an easel is not available, use a countertop or desk for the Painting Learning Center.

1. Cover the countertop or desk with newspaper.
2. Put four rolled sheets of 18-by-24-inch paper in a container (3-pound coffee can) on the counter.
3. Put the paint jars and brushes on a tray on the counter.

To care for the paints and brushes, the last child who paints each day should wash the brushes, put the lids on the paints, and clean up any spilled paint.

To take care of the completed paintings:

1. Each child can hang up his or her own painting by using two clothespins clipped to a wire under a chalkboard or above the countertop.

2. Using a bookcase
   a. Attach two wires 50 inches long across the back of a bookcase that is at least 50 inches long by 40 inches high.
   b. Cover the back of the bookcase with paper (bulletin board roll paper 36 inches wide can be stapled over the top wire).
   c. Clip four clothespins to each wire. Two paintings can be pinned to each wire. (There will be a maximum of four paintings daily if you have four groups.)

Painting Center Ideas

1. Use different media, such as watercolors, fingerpaints, marking pens, tempera, and sponges.
2. Use different colors and sizes of paper.
3. Choose your own subjects to paint.
4. Paint specific subjects.
5. Write a few sentences about the painting.

The Coordination Learning Center

Set up two or three manipulative activities that will help develop coordination (mainly hand-eye and small-muscle).

Coordination Center Ideas

1. Pour dry materials such as rice or beans from one small pitcher (two-cup size) to another over a tray.

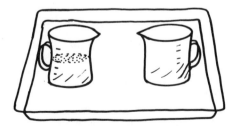

2. Use an eye dropper to transfer water, one drop at a time, from one small bottle to another.
3. Use tongs to transfer beads or walnuts (one at a time) from one bowl to another.

4. Hammer tacks or nails into a soft piece of wood or a stump.

5. Use pegboards to make designs, count number of pegs in a row, and so on.

6. Use a paper punch to punch holes in 3-by-5-inch index cards or colored construction paper. Make designs by gluing the punched-out pieces on paper.

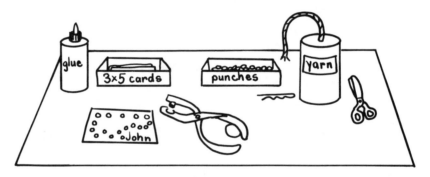

7. Use a baster to transfer colored water (use a few drops of food coloring or tempera paint) from one small dishpan or jar to another.

8. Put six or more padlocks in one box. Put matching keys in another box. Child locks and unlocks the matching ones.

9. Use commercial sewing cards, or child can make his or her own with index cards and a paper punch. Child can thread a bobby pin with yarn to sew.

10. Use a hand eggbeater to mix a few drops of detergent in a dishpan.

The Handwriting Learning Center

Use the chalkboard for this center. Use a wide permanent black marking pen and a yardstick to draw lines on a 6-foot section of the chalkboard. Draw horizontal lines approximately 2 inches apart, alternating a solid line with a broken line (similar to commercial writing paper). These guidelines provide a structured area in which the child can practice writing skills.

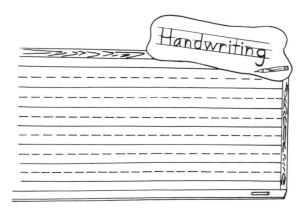

Handwriting Center Ideas

1. The teacher writes words or sentences on the chalkboard with colored chalk. The child copies the words under the example given with yellow chalk. The child erases his or her own words only. After the child has written words on the chalkboard, he or she writes the same words on writing paper. (The child's work on paper will be better if he or she has an opportunity to practice first on the chalkboard.)

2. Attach teacher-made tagboard letters or word cards to the chalkboard with magnets or masking tape. The child copies the words with chalk, then writes the words on paper.

3. Using a paintbrush and a small can of water, copy teacher-written words on the chalkboard. (Children love to watch their words disappear.)

4. Divide the chalkboard into eight boxes (approximately 6 inches square). Child can use a word chart to write a word and draw a picture in each box.

5. Use magnetic letters on the chalkboard. The child can put all of the upper-case letters of the alphabet on the chalkboard, then write the matching lower-case letters below them.

6. Use an overhead projector and practice writing on transparencies with a marking pen.

7. Practice writing letters with a finger in a dishpan filled with sand.

8. Cover a table with plastic or fingerpaint paper. Practice writing with a finger and chocolate pudding or fingerpaint.

9. Write a poem and illustrate it.

10. Use a story starter, such as, "If I had $5 I would . . . ," and write a story.

11. Use a big chart book for "Daily News." Child writes his or her name, date, and a sentence or two of his or her news.

The Computer Learning Center

A computer can be used in numerous ways at a learning center. The extent to which you use one will depend on the kind of computer, types of software available, and the computer's accessibility.

Scheduling the Computer

1. Ideally, the computer should be set up at a learning center (near an electrical outlet) for an eight-day period. The child uses the computer at his or her regularly scheduled learning center time.

2. The child could be sent to use the computer in your school's media center or computer lab during his or her learning center time.
   a. Advanced planning is required with a school support person (media specialist, parent aide, or older student aide) to schedule and direct the student.
   b. Rules for leaving the classroom and using the computer should be established with the children.

Advantages of Using a Computer

1. Each child has an opportunity to use the computer for approximately 30 minutes during an eight-day period, eliminating teacher scheduling of turns.

2. A variety of skill lessons can be presented and reinforced.

3. Children enjoy using it and catch on very rapidly to the directions.

4. It becomes a manipulative learning center instead of a pencil and paper activity.

5. It requires a minimum amount of record keeping.

Other Learning Centers

Reading, math, science, art, social studies, spelling, and music activities will vary greatly depending on the grade level and the skills you are teaching.

1. These learning centers may be placed at different areas depending on the activities.
2. Diversify these learning centers through the use of:
   a. manipulatives—pocket charts, bulletin board matching activities, flannel board sets, gameboards, science kits.
   b. audiovisual aids—filmstrip viewers, tape recorders, records.
   c. electronic learning aids—many commercial ones are available in most toy catalogs (You might even be able to borrow these from students for an eight-day period.)

HOW TO KEEP THE LEARNING CENTER ORDERLY

Cover the center's table with paper, especially if glue or other messy materials are being used. Write numbers with a black marking pen on one-inch squares of orange construction paper and glue or tape these numbers on the envelopes and containers to correspond with the numbers on the direction file folder. The orange numbers are visible and easy for the child to follow in sequential order.

Draw around the containers, books, games, and charts with a black marking pen so that the outlines act as boundaries. The child can then keep the materials in place when they are not in use.

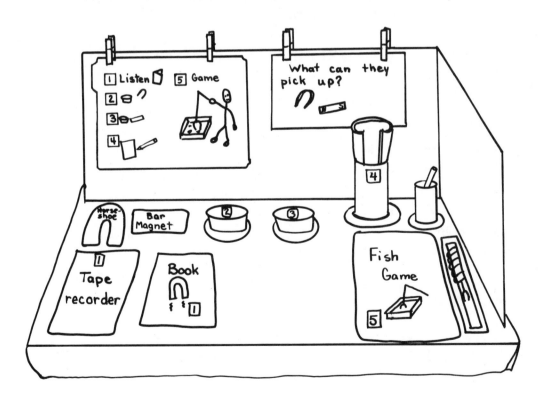

HOW TO MAINTAIN LEARNING CENTER MATERIALS DAILY

Put only enough consumable materials in a learning center for one day's use. For example, if you have four groups you would put in four papers. Children will occasionally take more than one paper if they make a mistake, so stress that there are only enough materials for each child.

Check the learning center daily and add the necessary materials. (Student aides can help with this job.)

HOW TO SAVE TIME IN SETTING UP LEARNING CENTERS

1. Since you may initially spend time setting up learning centers after school, you can give yourself a break by starting a new set of learning centers on Tuesday rather than Monday.

2. Plan an art project or a film, which requires little teacher participation, during the afternoon. Use the time to set up learning centers.

3. Recruit a parent or student aide to help set up in the afternoon while you are teaching a whole group activity. (You can prepare in advance by having the materials for each learning center placed at their respective area.)

4. Let the students help (this will vary according to age group). If you are sharing learning centers with another teacher, you can easily exchange at the end of the eight-day period. The eight individual learning centers can be carried on trays or boxes by eight children from one classroom to the other.

HELPFUL CONTAINERS FOR LEARNING CENTER MATERIALS

Mailbox Unit

Materials needed:

Black permanent marking pen

One clean half-gallon milk carton for each child

Stapler and staples

Two-inch-wide masking tape or duct tape

One 3½-by-2-inch piece of construction paper for each carton
(use a different color for each row of cartons)

Scissors

To make the mailbox unit:

1. Cut off the tops of the milk cartons.
2. Lay six cartons, with the opening facing front, side-by-side in a row.

3. Staple the sides of two cartons together. Continue stapling cartons until you have all six in a row, as shown in the illustration.

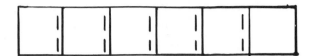

4. Staple additional rows of six cartons until you have enough for your entire class (one carton per child).

5. Stack one row of six cartons on top of another row of six cartons. Staple the bottom of the first row to the top of the second row. Continue to staple one additional row at a time until all of the rows are together in a complete unit.

6. Wrap strips of two-inch-wide masking tape or duct tape around the entire unit three or more times to strengthen the unit.

7. Fold one piece of 3½-by-2-inch construction paper in half. Write a child's name on the bottom half of the paper. Staple the top inch of the paper inside the top of the carton. The inch with the name will hang down over the opening of the carton as illustrated.

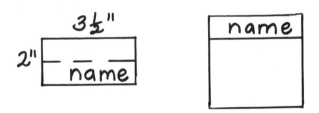

8. Complete the top row of six cartons with the same color of paper. Use a different color for each row of six cartons.

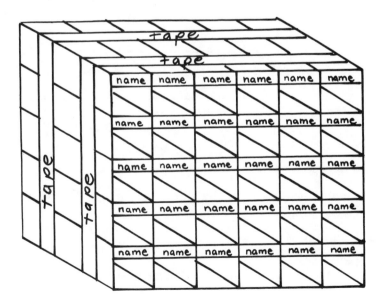

Ways to use the mailbox unit:

1. The child can put his or her seatwork and boardwork papers in his or her own mailbox when finished with them. Later in the morning schedule (at makeup time), ask one row of children (for example, the red row of mailboxes) to bring their papers to you. You can quickly check to see if the work is finished and if the child's name is on it. If the work is not complete, the child can join the other children doing makeup work.

2. The mailbox can be used for finished graded work. When you have a break, distribute a set of graded papers that the children can put in their mailboxes. If you have an older student helper, he or she can put the papers in the mailboxes. This method makes dismissal time much smoother, because the children can be called by rows (one color of the mailbox rows) to get their papers.

Stacking Unit

A child can put his or her finished seatwork and boardwork papers in a series of trays of a stacking unit.

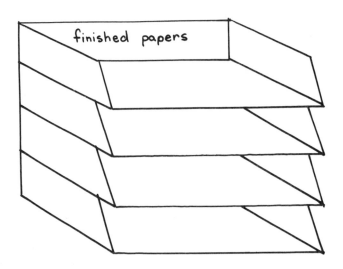

Go Home Box

Materials needed:

One empty soft drink bottle box (kind that holds 24 bottles),
   11 by 16 by 10 inches

One pint of paint

Two-inch paintbrush

One-half yard of 18-inch-wide Con-Tact paper

Tagboard letters (4-inch capital letters and 2½-inch
lowercase letters)

Pencil

Scissors

To make the Go Home box:

1. Paint the outside of the box, except the bottom side.
2. Tracing tagboard letters, write "Go Home" on Con-Tact paper.
3. After the box is dry, put the words "Go Home" on one side of it. The Go Home box is an excellent catchall for learning center projects that are too big for a mailbox, notes, books, small "show and share" items, eyeglasses, and so on. The Go Home box can be sorted out daily at dismissal time.

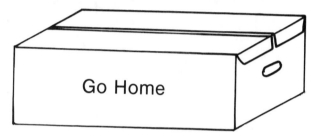

Manila Envelope

Ways to use a manila envelope:

1. Fold over the top flap of a 10-by-13-inch manila envelope.
2. Make a 3-inch diagonal cut from each of the top corners.
3. Fold the cut section under and staple.

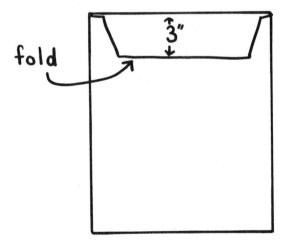

4. The envelope can be attached to the top of a desk divider with a clothespin. It can hold 9-by-12-inch paper, puzzles, and books.

5. The student activity page may be attached to the front, enabling the child to see the content.

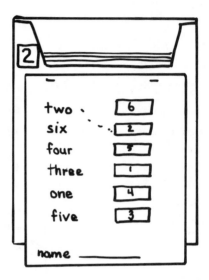

Coffee Cans

One-, two-, and three-pound coffee cans can hold many different sizes of paper, pencils, and other materials.

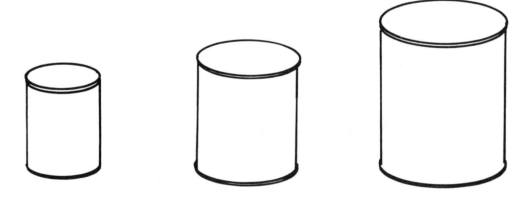

To make a coffee can unit:

1. Cut out the top and bottom of three three-pound coffee cans with a can opener.
2. Cover the cans with Con-Tact paper or spray paint.
3. Stack the cans.
4. Tie the cans together by wrapping heavy twine through the insides of the cans joining 1 and 2, 1 and 3, and 2 and 3.

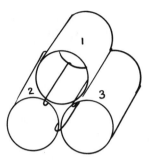

Ways to use a coffee can unit:

You may vary the size of the unit by adding more coffee cans. This unit can hold materials of various sizes (especially 12-by-18-inch paper). A can unit can be used at a learning center to keep materials organized in a minimal amount of space. Boardwork and seatwork papers can be placed in a can unit in a central location (such as a bookcase dividing the room), making them accessible to both areas.

Other Cans, Tubs, and Trays

Orange juice cans and soup cans are ideal for holding scissors, pencils, crayons, marking pens, and many other supplies.

Margarine tubs are excellent for brass fasteners, paper clips, tacks, game-board markers, and cards.

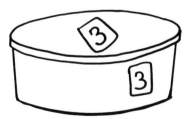

Trays of various sizes and shapes are great for messy activities. Use them for liquid and dry pouring, basting, painting, gluing, working with clay, and working with papier-mâché.

4. Science Learning Center Units

The Five Senses

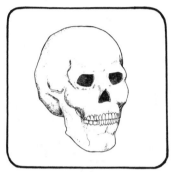

The Human Body

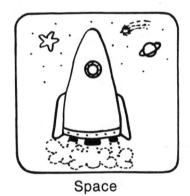

Space

Plants

Dinosaurs

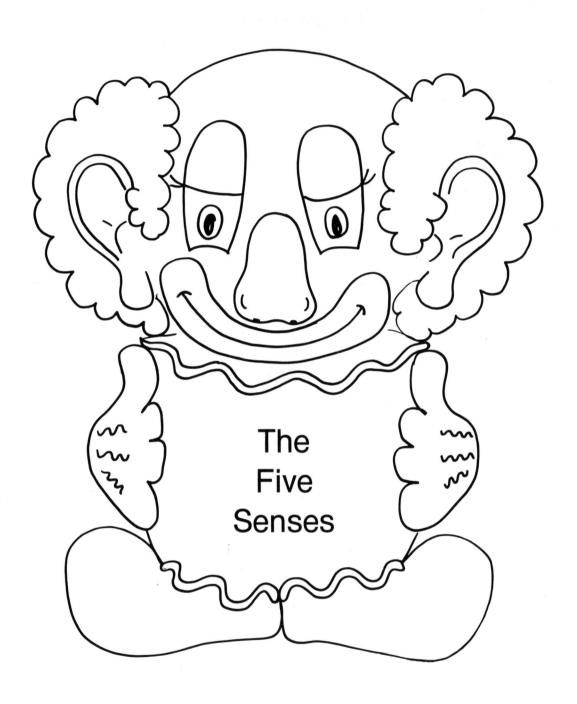

The
Five
Senses

SENSES ALIVE!

Date _____

Dear Parent,

"One, two, three, four, five. Let your senses come alive!" Your child will be encouraged to use his or her senses in various ways at the new Five Senses Learning Centers.

At one of the Touch Centers children will remove their shoes and use only their feet to identify objects that have been sewn into socks. At another Touch Center they will use their fingers to paint.

The children will smell eight different scents in jars at the Smell Center.

Listening skills will be needed to follow tape-recorded directions at the Hearing Center.

At the Sight Center the children will have an opportunity to look at things through binoculars and other lenses. Then they will make a set of "Look-for" cards. You can easily extend this activity at your home.

Tasting foods will be a favorite experience at the Taste Center.

While participating in the Five Senses Learning Centers your child will learn to record information in many different ways, including on graphs.

During the next two weeks your child is welcome to bring books, records, games, and similar materials pertaining to the five senses.

Thank you for your continued support.

Sincerely,

Your child's teacher

GROUP ACTIVITIES

Send the letter requesting parent help home with the students.

Prior to going on the "smell" walking trip, divide the students into small groups. Appoint a recorder for each group (a parent can record for younger students). The recorder will write down the odors identified by his or her group (provide a ditto master on a clipboard and a pencil for each recorder).

After returning from the trip each group can compare the odors identified on its list. Compile a class list of the number of smells and the area they are found in. Creative writing can be encouraged by giving each student a copy of his or her group recorder's list (use as key vocabulary).

Prepare for the "touch" walking trip by dividing the students into small groups. Appoint a leader for each group. The leader can carry a grocery bag containing a supply of newsprint (approximately four sheets per student) and a small shoebox of crayons with paper removed (two per student). The leader will pass out the materials at a specific area of interest. The students will make crayon rubbings of different textures, such as a sidewalk, tires, tree bark, and bricks.

As follow-up activities you can exchange papers and guess what objects were used for the rubbings, discuss how various textures felt, compile a class list of descriptive words (rough, bumpy, smooth, soft, hard, slippery), or use the word list for creative writing.

WE NEED YOUR HELP!

Date _____

Dear Parent,

    Our class has been learning to use the five senses. During the next two weeks we will go on two different walking trips to develop better awareness of our senses.

    On _____ at _____ we will go on a "smell" walking trip. We will see how many odors we can identify in the cafeteria and the surrounding school area.

    A "touch" walking trip will enable us to use our fingers to discover a variety of textures. We will go on the "touch" walking trip on _____ _____ at _____. The walk will encompass the following area:

_____

_____.

    The students will be divided into small groups for the trips. Group size will be determined by the number of parent volunteers.

    Please check and sign the lower portion of this note if you would be willing to help us.

    Thank you for your continued support.

Sincerely,

Your child's teacher

---------------------------- cut along here ----------------------------

_____ Yes, I would be able to go on the "smell" walking trip on _____ _____ at _____ .

_____ Yes, I would be able to go on the "touch" walking trip on _____ _____ at _____ .

signed _____ phone _____

Please return this note by _____ . You will be contacted for definite arrangements.

BOARDWORK ACTIVITIES

1. Develop word bank charts for each of the five senses. Use them as references for creative writing.
2. Use the following column format to create category lists:

   I Touch   I See   I Hear   I Taste   I Smell

   a. Older students write words in each column.
   b. Younger students draw pictures.
3. Create class patterning books in which each student does one or two pages that are stapled into the books. Some ideas are

   I'm not as soft as a _____. A _____ is softer than I am.

   I'm not as cold as a _____. A _____ is colder than I am.
4. Use an eight-box format for these dictionary-pictionary ideas:
   a. Older student: Find eight things you can hear (touch, see, taste, smell) and write words in each box describing the sound (feeling, sight, taste, smell).
   b. Younger student: Find eight things you can hear (touch, see, taste, smell) and draw the pictures.
5. Make five big charts (use one chart for each sense) and have students cut and paste magazine pictures onto each chart.
6. Make pictures using 12-by-18-inch construction paper, glue, and a collection of several different textures, for example, sandpaper, yarn, felt, corrugated cardboard, tissue paper, cotton, and fur. Students write a few sentences describing the picture.
7. Write sentence strips (prepare several laminated tagboard strips). Students copy four or more sentences (use four-row format) and write the correct sense on the back. Some ideas are

   "Tom ate an ice-cream cone." (taste)
   "The thorns are sharp." (touch)
   "Our flag is red, white, and blue." (sight)
   "Chocolate cookies are baking in the oven." (smell)
   "My alarm clock rang." (hearing)
8. Write experience stories following the "smell" walk using
   a. A copy of group recorder's list for key vocabulary
   b. "Smells I Like"; "Smells I Don't Like"
9. Make a class book of crayon rubbings following the "touch" walk. Each student can label his or her rubbings or write a few sentences about them.

FIVE SENSES CENTER MARKER

Distribute copies of the clown marker to the students. The students can cut out their markers and place them near the Five Senses Learning Centers.

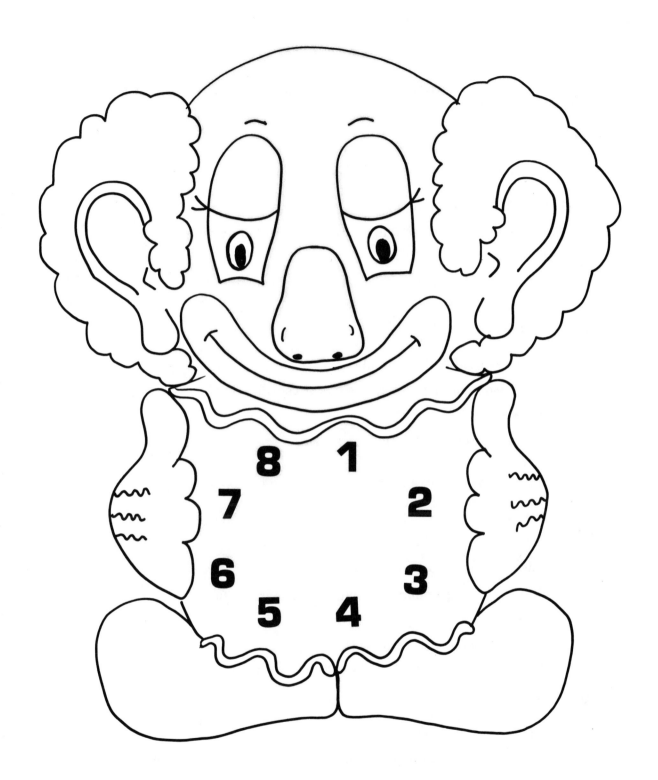

LEARNING CENTERS LIST

The following learning centers encourage the student to use his or her five senses. Each is described in detail later.

Taste Center

(A bulletin board is used with this center.)

Content areas: Science, math

Skills: Observing, classifying, graphing, communicating

Activities:

1. Taste and record foods on a student activity page.
2. Record favorite tastes on a bulletin board.

Our Five Senses Center

Content areas: Reading, handwriting

Skills: Listening, matching, fine-motor coordination

Activities:

1. Listen to a story about the five senses.
2. Write a poem.
3. Match the senses on a student activity page.

Touch Center
(Feet)

Content areas: Science, handwriting

Skills: Observing, communicating, tactile perception

Activities:

1. Feel objects in a sock game with your feet.
2. Record objects' names on a student activity page.

Smell Center

Content areas: Science, reading

Skills: Observing, matching, communicating, olfactory perception

Activities:

1. Use your nose to match the food jars with the food cards.
2. Record smells identified with words and pictures.

Touch Center
(Fingers)

Content areas: Art, handwriting

Skills: Fine-motor coordination, creative writing, creating

Activities:

1. Use fingerpaints.
2. Use two student activity pages for "I Like to Touch _____" creative writing and pictures.

Hearing Center

Content areas: Reading, science

Skills: Auditory perception, matching, observing

Activities:

1. Match the sound cans.
2. Listen to story about sounds.
3. Follow the tape recorded directions to complete a student activity page.

Tasty Ice-Cream-Cones Center
(Open-Ended Activity)

Content area: Teacher's choice

Skills: Teacher's choice

Activities:

1. Play teacher-made game.
2. Make ice-cream cone flashcards.

Sight

Content areas: Science, reading, handwriting

Skills: Observing, using reference materials, communicating, fine-motor coordination

Activities:

1. Look at objects through a variety of lenses.
2. Make a "Look for _____" envelope.
3. Copy six "Look for _____" cards and complete assignments.

TEACHER'S DIRECTIONS FOR THE TASTE CENTER

Content areas: Science, math

Skills: Observing, classifying, graphing, communicating

Materials needed:

Bulletin board

Teacher-made tasting game

Teacher-made food picture cards

Thumbtacks

Containers

Four 1½-by-3-inch construction-paper cards per student

Pencil

Crayons

Copies of student activity page

Materials preparation:

1. Make "Our Favorite Tastes" bulletin board as shown on the file folder directions page.

2. Make food picture cards for the bulletin board:
   - Sour: dill pickle, lemon
   - Salty: potato chip, pretzel
   - Bitter: bitter chocolate, orange peel
   - Sweet: jelly bean, mint candy

3. Make a tasting game:
   a. Use eight identical containers, such as small margarine tubs or baby food jars. Number the containers 1 through 8.
   b. Daily put four servings (if you have four groups) of each of the foods shown on the food picture cards in the eight different containers (follow the exact order listed on the student activity page).

Directions for file folder activities:

Activity 1

1. The student tastes the food in container 1 and records his or her reaction by coloring the Happy Face (I Like It) or the Sad Face (I Don't Like It) on the student activity page. Then the student tastes the food in container 2 and records it. Next, the student chooses his or her favorite taste and writes an X by it in the "My Favorites" column.

2. The child tastes and records the remaining foods in order.

Activity 2

1. The student writes his or her name on four construction-paper cards.

2. The child tacks his or her cards above his or her favorite taste choice in each of the four basic taste groups on the bulletin board.

Follow-Up Activity

The bulletin board becomes a bar graph. Students can make comparisons on different days and the final day of the Five Senses Learning Centers.

Taste

1

Taste the foods.
Mark the ditto.

2

Put your name on 4 cards.
Tack it above your favorite food
for each kind of taste.

Our Favorite Tastes

Number of Students:

4 basic tastes: sour   salty   bitter   sweet

File Folder Directions

Taste

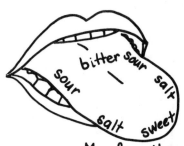

bitter sour
sour salt
salt sweet

My favorites
Put an X.

Basic Taste:	Food:	I like it.	I don't like it.	My favorites Put an X.
sour	1. pickle	🙂	🙁	
	2. lemon	🙂	🙁	
salty	3. pretzel	🙂	🙁	
	4. potato chip	🙂	🙁	
bitter	5. bitter chocolate	🙂	🙁	
	6. orange peel	🙂	🙁	
sweet	7. jelly bean	🙂	🙁	
	8. mint	🙂	🙁	

TEACHER'S DIRECTIONS FOR THE OUR FIVE SENSES CENTER

Content areas: Reading, handwriting

Skills: Listening, matching, fine-motor coordination

Materials needed:

Tape recorder

Cassette tape

Pencil

Crayons

Handwriting paper

Copies of student activity page

Teacher-made example of poem

A book about the five senses such as Aliki, *My Five Senses*, Thomas Y. Crowell Co., New York, 1962

Materials preparation

1. Tape record the book you have chosen for this center.
2. Write on paper the following poem by Carol Poppe as a sample:

"Senses Alive!"
One, two, three, four, five,
Let your senses come alive!
Use your mouth and ears and nose,
Don't forget your eyes and toes.

(You may prefer to draw pictures of the parts of the body instead of writing the words.)

Directions for file folder activities:

Activity 1

The student listens to the story.

Activity 2

The student copies the poem about the five senses.

Activity 3

The student matches the senses on the student activity page. (Older students may write the word under each picture.)

Our Five Senses

1 Listen to the book.

2 Copy the poem.

3 Match the Senses ditto.

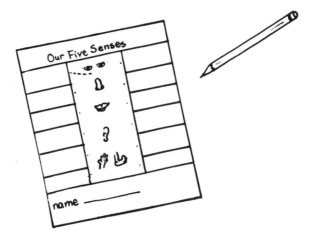

File Folder Directions

Our Five Senses

see

smell

taste

hear

touch

More than one sense may be used.

Name _____

Student Activity Page

85

TEACHER'S DIRECTIONS FOR THE TOUCH (FEET) CENTER

Content areas: Science, handwriting

Skills: Observing, communicating, tactile perception

Materials needed:

Teacher-made sock game and box

Copies of student activity page

Posterboard

Pencil

Crayons

Materials preparation:

1. Make a sock game.
   a. Collect eight different objects (for example, a sponge, an eraser, a ball, a crayon, a small glue bottle, a clothespin, a small ruler, a large marking pen).
   b. Put one object in each of eight large socks, then sew the socks shut near the top.
   c. Staple or sew a 2-inch square of heavy paper near the top of each sock.
   d. Label the eight squares of paper (1 through 8) with a crayon.
   e. Provide a box for the socks.
2. Make a reference chart. Write the words for the eight objects on a sheet of posterboard.

Directions for file folder activities:

Activity 1

The student empties the sock box on the floor. He or she removes his or her shoes. Using only the feet, the child feels the object in each sock and tries to identify it.

Activity 2

The student writes the name of each object on the corresponding sock on the student activity page (reference chart is optional). The student may color the socks on the student activity page.

Touch

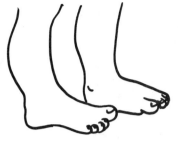

 Take off your shoes. Feel the socks with <u>only</u> your feet.

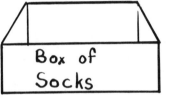

2 Write what you felt in each sock.

Touch

Name _____

1

2

3

4

5

6

7

8

Student Activity Page

TEACHER'S DIRECTIONS FOR THE SMELL CENTER

Content areas: Science, reading

Skills: Observing, matching, communicating, olfactory perception

Materials needed:

Teacher-made "smell" game and box

Teacher-made cards

Paper

Pencil

Crayons

Materials preparation:

1. Make the "smell" game. Cover eight baby food jars or similar containers with Con-Tact paper. Label the jars and the lids 1 through 8 with a permanent marking pen. Put a different food or spice in each jar and cover with the lid.
2. Make the cards.
   a. Make a set of eight tagboard cards with the matching picture or name of each of the eight foods in the jars. Laminate the cards or cover them with clear Con-Tact paper to protect them.
   b. Provide a box for the jars and cards.

Directions for file folder activities:

Activity 1

1. The student lays the food cards on a table.
2. He or she takes the lid off of the first jar, smells the jar, sets it on the matching card, and replaces the lid.
3. The child continues to match the jars and cards in sequence.

Activity 2

1. The student folds the paper into an eight-box format.
2. He or she numbers the boxes 1 through 8.
3. The student writes the corresponding word from the card in each box.
4. He or she draws the matching picture in each box.

Smell

1 Use your nose to match the jars with the cards.

2 Write the words and draw the pictures of each thing you smelled on 8-box paper.

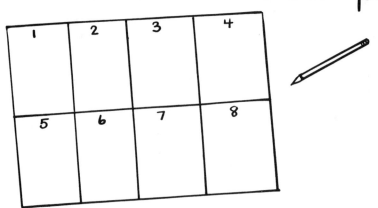

File Folder Directions

90

TEACHER'S DIRECTIONS FOR
THE TOUCH (FINGERS) CENTER

Content areas: Art, handwriting

Skills: Fine-motor coordination, creative writing, creating

Materials needed:

A medium for fingerpainting: fingerpaint, chocolate pudding, vanilla pudding (food coloring optional)

Paper for fingerpainting

Paint container

Cookie sheet or tray

Newspaper or plastic garbage bag

Old shirt

Copies of the student activity pages

Pencil

Scissors

Paste

Crayons

Materials preparation:

1. Cover a table with a plastic garbage bag or newspaper.
2. Put the tray and the paint container on the table.

Directions for file folder activities:

Activity 1

1. The student puts on the shirt.
2. He or she lays the fingerpaint paper in the tray.
3. He or she fingerpaints using a small amount of the medium.
4. The student puts the finished painting in the prearranged area to dry.
5. He or she cleans up the area and him- or herself.

Activity 2

1. The student colors the hands on part one of the student activity page.
2. He or she cuts out the index fingers.

Activity 3

1. The student draws a picture on part two of the student activity page of what he or she likes to touch.
2. He or she writes a word describing the picture.
3. The student pastes the edge of part one to the edge of part two.

Optional Activity

Older students may write an "I Like to Touch" story.

Touch

1 Fingerpaint.

2 What is your favorite thing to touch? Do dittos.

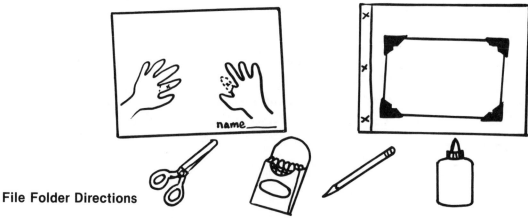

name____

File Folder Directions

92

What do you like to touch ?

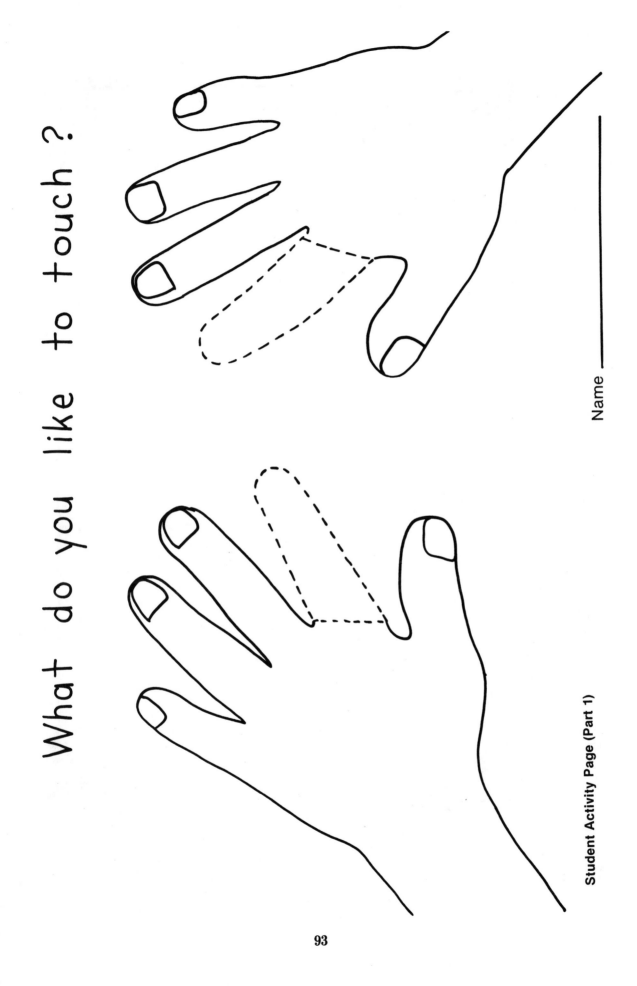

Name _____

Student Activity Page (Part 1)

I like to touch _____.

Here it is.

X Put paste here. X

X

TEACHER'S DIRECTIONS FOR THE HEARING CENTER

Content areas: Reading, science

Skills: Auditory perception, matching, observing

Materials needed:

Teacher-made matching "sounds" game and box

Copies of student activity page

Tape recorder

Cassette tape

Pencil

Crayons

Book about sounds, such as Podendorf, Illa, *Sounds All About*, Children's Press, Chicago, 1970

Materials preparation:

1. Make the game.
   a. Use eight identical opaque containers with lids, such as small margarine tubs, potato chip cans, or film canisters. Fill pairs of containers with balls, sand, beans, and pennies.
   b. Make the lids opaque by putting dark Con-Tact paper or construction paper on the inside of the lids. Permanently seal the lids with masking tape so the student cannot see the contents.
   c. Using a marking pen, make container outlines on four posterboard squares (two container outlines per square).
   d. Provide a box for the game.
   e. Prepare a cassette tape of the book and the following directions for the student activity page:
      • Write your name on the "hearing" ditto.
      • Listen to the first sound (a bell). Write "1" under the picture that is making that sound.
      • Continue directions in a similar manner, giving the remaining sounds shown on the student activity page in random order.

Directions for file folder activities:

Activity 1

The student shakes the sound containers, matches the pairs that are alike, and places them on the posterboard squares.

Activity 2

The student listens to the cassette tape of the book.

Activity 3

He or she follows the tape-recorded directions for the student activity page.

Optional Activities

1. Younger students might color the pictures.
2. Older students might color or mark pictures in a specific way following teacher-taped directions. For example, "color the animal brown," "put an X on the ball," and so on.
3. Older students might write the word under each picture.

Hearing

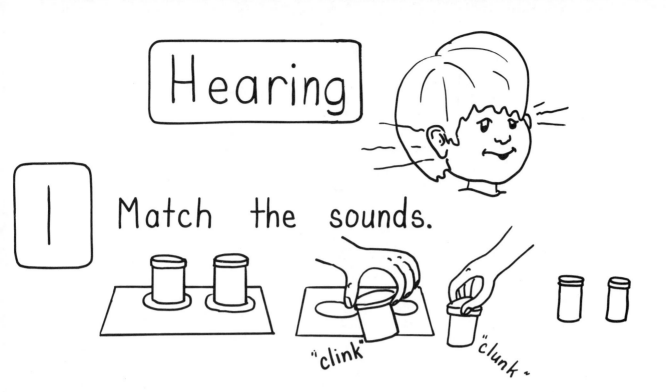

1 Match the sounds.

"clink"   "clunk"

2 Listen to the book.

Sounds **2**

3 Do the ditto with the tape.

File Folder Directions

Hearing

Name _____

___

___

___

___

___

___

___

___

Listen with your ears.

Student Activity Page

98

TEACHER'S DIRECTIONS FOR THE TASTY ICE-CREAM-CONE CENTER

Content area: Teacher's choice

Skills: Teacher's choice

Materials needed:

Teacher-made ice-cream-cone game and box

Copies (on heavy paper) of student activity page
  (two per student)

Pencil

Scissors

Crayons

Envelope

Materials preparation:

1. To make the ice-cream-cone game, use two copies of the student activity page to make eight flashcards to reinforce or review a skill. Some ideas are math problems, contractions, color words, compound words, and ice-cream-cone flavors.

2. Provide a box for the game.

Directions for file folder activities:

Activity 1
The student plays the game.

Activity 2

The student uses two copies of the student activity page to make eight flashcards referring to the game. He or she colors, cuts, and places the flashcards in an envelope. The student may use the flashcards with a friend.

Tasty Ice Cream Cones

1 Play the game.

2 Make your own flashcards.

File Folder Directions

TEACHER'S DIRECTIONS FOR THE SIGHT CENTER

Content areas: Science, reading, handwriting

Skills: Observing, using reference materials, communicating, fine-motor coordination

Materials needed:

Binoculars, microscope, magnifying glass, or other lenses

A box of assorted objects to observe with lenses

Teacher-made "Look-for" cards and box

Copies (on heavy paper) of student activity page

Three 4-by-6-inch index cards per student

Stapler and staples

Pencil

Scissors

Crayons

Materials preparation:

1. Set up this center near a window.
2. To make the Look-for cards:
   a. Write 10 Look-for assignments on individual 4-by-6-inch index cards (laminate or cover the cards with clear Con-Tact paper). Choose assignments that the student can complete easily by referring to room charts, name cards, and the like. Encourage the students to be good detectives to find their answers. Some ideas for Look-for cards are:
      • Look for four months that end with *r*.
      • Look for six boys with freckles.
      • Look for children who have birthdays in July.
      • Look for girls who have first names that start with *J*.
      • Look for three things in the room that start with *p*.
   b. Provide a box for the cards.

Directions for file folder activities:

Activity 1

The student uses the lenses to look at a variety of objects on the center table and through the window.

Activity 2

1. The student folds, cuts, and staples the student activity page into a Look-for envelope. (Coloring the envelope is optional.)
2. He or she copies six of the teacher-made Look-for cards on three index cards using both sides.
3. He or she completes the Look-for assignments by writing the answers on the index cards.
4. The student puts the cards in the envelope.

Sight

1 Use your eyes to look a special way.

2 Make a "Look for..." envelope. Copy 6 cards and look for those things.

1. Cut.

2. Staple.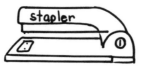

File Folder Directions

104

1. Make the envelope.

2. Copy the words from 6 cards onto 3 cards. (Use front and back.)

3. Write the answers on the cards so they will show in the glasses.

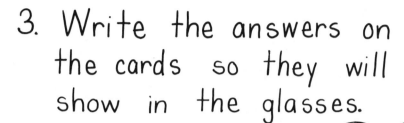

___fold here___ _ _ _ _ _ _ _ _ _ _

name

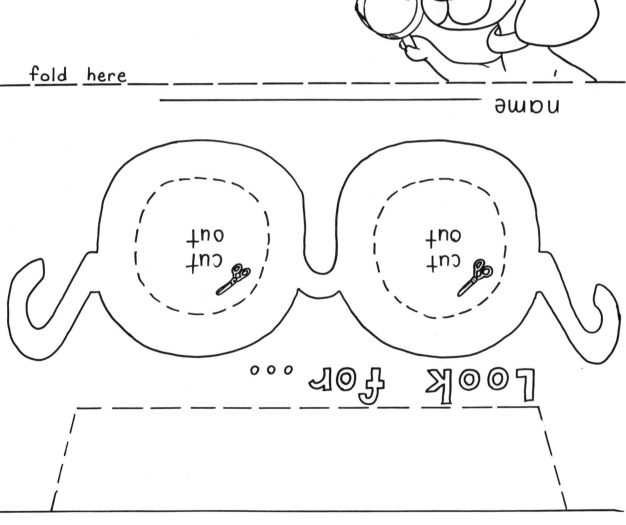

cut
out

cut
out

Look for ...

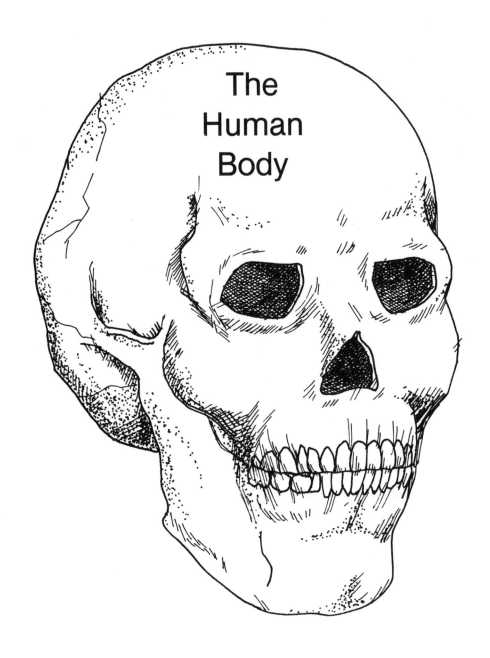

The
Human
Body

ALL ABOUT ME

Date _____

Dear Parent,

The human body is the theme of our new learning centers. Your child will become more aware of his or her body, with emphasis on the heart, bones, skin, teeth, hands, and feet.

At the Heart Center your child will have an opportunity to listen to his or her own heart with a stethoscope. The child will record his or her heart rate after standing, walking, and running.

Anticipate receiving a huge roll of paper with your child's body outlined on it. Please find a place to display this picture because your child will have worked very hard labeling the body parts.

At the Teeth Center your child will chew a plaque-disclosing tablet and view the results in a mirror. Your child may want to brush his or her teeth more frequently after seeing the plaque!

A magnifying glass will be used to observe skin, hair, fingertips, and bones. Please send any clean and washed animal bones for our collection.

At the Math Center your child will measure his or her hand and foot, as well as several objects. Encourage your child to continue this activity at home.

Our "Read All About Us" bulletin board will feature student-created books. You are welcome to visit to read the books and see all of our centers.

Thank you for your continued support.

Sincerely,

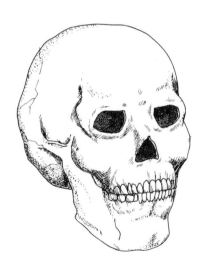

_____

Your child's teacher

GROUP ACTIVITIES

The purpose of this group activity is to help students understand the circulatory system.

Prepare students by giving them background information about the heart's part in the circulatory system through the use of audiovisual aids or books such as Showers, Paul, *Hear Your Heart*, Thomas Y. Crowell Co., New York, 1968 or Weart, Edith L., *The Story of Your Blood*, Coward, McCann, and Geoghegan, New York, 1960.

It would also be helpful to develop a vocabulary chart listing terms, such as blood, vein, artery, heart, chambers, valves, lungs, oxygen, and carbon dioxide.

Materials needed:

Diagram of the heart drawn on a large floor mat

A large area such as a gymnasium, outdoor playground,
    or parking lot

Masking tape

Red and blue chalk

One sheet of 6-by-6-inch red paper per student

One sheet of 6-by-6-inch blue paper per student

Pencils

Scissors

Six shoe boxes: three covered with red paper or painted red and
    three covered with blue paper or painted blue

Procedure:

1. Set up the area in the shape of the circulatory system shown in the diagram. (Note that there is only one lung shown on the diagram to facilitate smooth group movement.) The vein paths may be drawn with blue chalk and the artery paths with red chalk. Place the shoe boxes in the appropriate areas (two at the head, two at the feet, two in the lung).

2. Give the students one sheet each of red and blue paper.
    a. The students fold the blue paper into fourths then cut it into four pieces. They label each piece "CO_2" or "carbon dioxide" (the blue paper represents blood with carbon dioxide).
    b. The students fold the red paper into fourths and cut it into four pieces. They label each piece "O_2" or "oxygen" (the red paper represents blood with oxygen).
    c. Place the blue squares in the blue shoe boxes at the head and feet areas. Place the red squares in the red shoe box in the lung area.

3. Select students for the following jobs and explain their roles:
   - Two students per valve (eight total); they will use their arms to gently stop each student before he or she enters and leaves a chamber of the heart.
   - Two students at the head; they will hold the shoe boxes
   - Two students at the lung; they will hold the shoe boxes
   - Two students at the feet; they will hold the shoe boxes

   The remaining students are divided into two groups (A and B). Group A represents blood traveling the path from the heart to the head and back to the heart. Group B represents blood traveling the path from the heart to the feet and back to the heart.

4. Begin the group activity by assigning the valve and shoe box holders to their positions.
   a. Take each group (A and B) on a demonstration walk while the opposite group watches.
   b. Next, both groups walk together through the heart simultaneously.
   c. Group A begins at the lung, where each student picks up a red oxygen card from the red shoe box holder. Then they continue on the path through the two chambers of the heart, following the red artery path to the head. When they reach the head, they drop the red oxygen card into the red shoe box and pick up a blue carbon dioxide card from the blue shoe box holder. They continue to follow the blue vein path to the heart. They reenter the heart and go to the lung to drop off their blue carbon dioxide card and pick up a red card. They continue this movement until all of the cards are gone (four times).
   d. Group B follows the same movement through the lungs and the heart, then continues on the red artery path to the feet and returns to the heart via the blue vein path. They will continue this movement until all the cards are gone (four times).

Follow-up activities:

1. Discuss these questions: "Does blood travel to other parts of the body? What parts?" "Have you ever seen blue blood? Why or why not?"
2. Write an experience story.
3. Make copies of the diagram and color them.

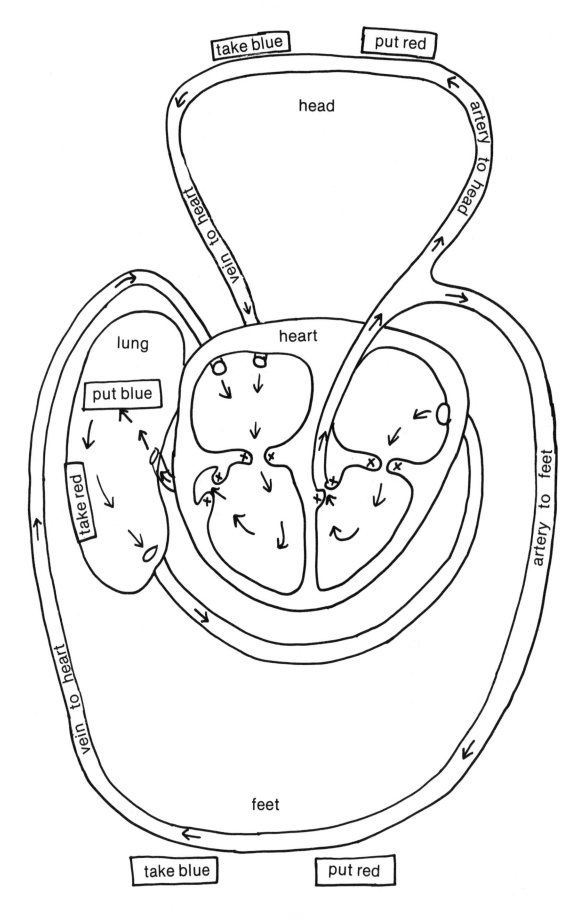

take blue

put red

head

artery to head

vein to heart

lung

heart

put blue

artery to feet

take red

vein to heart

feet

take blue

put red

BOARDWORK ACTIVITIES

1. Make picture-word body part reference charts.

2. Create body part riddles. For example, I am a pump. I am as big as your fist. I push blood. I beat. What am I? (heart)

   I cover your body. I have three layers. I keep out dirt and germs. What am I? (skin)

3. Write class body part shape books (nose, ear, foot, mouth).

4. Here are some pictionary-dictionary ideas:

   a. Using an eight-box format, find eight or sixteen body part words and illustrate them.

   b. An older student can use a two-column format to list "Animals with Endoskeletons" (fish, bird, mammal) or "Animals with Exoskeletons" (crab, lobster, barnacle).

   c. A younger student can use an eight-box format. Write the names of "Animals with Endoskeletons" or "Animals with Exoskeletons" on the board. Have the student copy the words, find them in a pictionary, and illustrate them.

5. Create dental health posters. Write and illustrate one dental health rule.

6. Design toothpaste flavor advertisements.

7. Write and illustrate eight snack foods that do not promote cavities. Examples are fresh fruits, crisp vegetables, nuts, popcorn, cheese, and milk.

8. Develop creative writing skills:

   "If I were the tooth fairy, I would _____."

   "If I were a skeleton on Halloween, I would _____."

   "If I had a neck like a _____, I would _____."

   "If I had ears like an elephant, I would _____."

   "If I had _____ feet, I would walk _____."
             (animal)

   "If I had _____, I would get a job _____."
          (body parts)

9. Write experience stories following a group activity.

HUMAN BODY CENTER MARKER

Distribute copies of the skull marker to the students. The students can cut out their markers and place them near the learning centers.

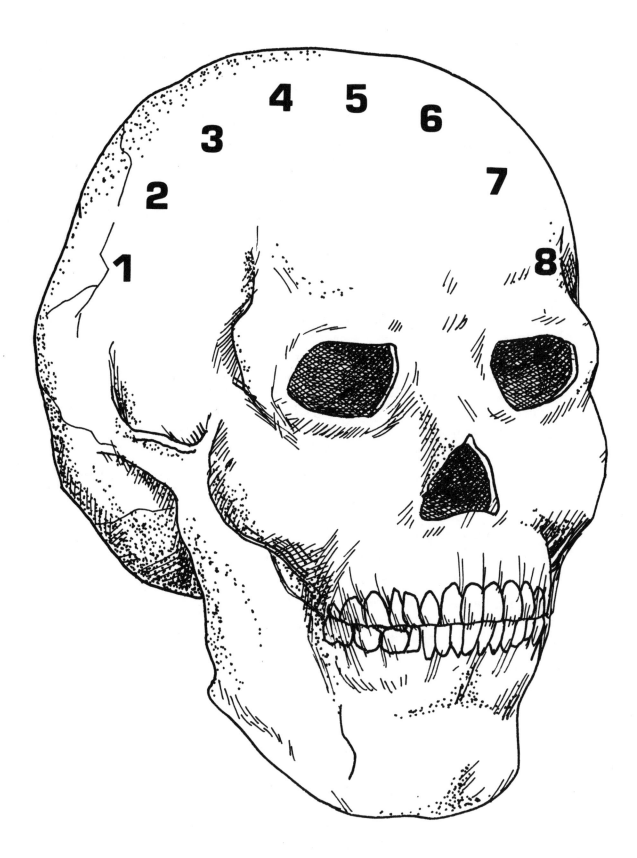

LEARNING CENTERS LIST

These learning centers present several parts of the human body.

All About Us Center

(A bulletin board is used with this center.)

Content areas: Reading, handwriting

Skills: Fine-motor coordination, communication

Activities:

1. Assemble pages for a book about yourself.
2. Write and illustrate sentences on the pages.

My Body Center

Content areas: Reading, art, handwriting

Skills: Fine-motor coordination, using references, creating

Activities:

1. Get a friend to trace around your body.
2. Write the names of body parts using a reference book.
3. Color the drawing of your body.

Heart Center

Content areas: Reading, science, math

Skills: Listening, measuring time, communicating

Activities:

1. Listen to the story about the heart.
2. Measure and record heartbeats on the student activity page.

Teeth Center

Content areas: Science, art, handwriting

Skills: Observing, creating, fine-motor coordination

Activities:

1. Chew a plaque-disclosing tablet, then look at your teeth in a mirror.
2. Draw a picture of your head. Color, cut out, and paste a toothbrush on the picture of your head.
3. Write down dental health rules.

Skin Center

Content areas: Science, art

Skills: Observing, creating

Activities:

1. Use a magnifying glass to look at your skin.
2. Make thumbprint pictures.

Bones Center

Content areas: Science, handwriting, art

Skills: Observing, creating, fine-motor coordination

Activities:

1. Use a magnifying glass to look at animal bones.
2. Write the names of the bones.
3. Draw a skeleton picture.

Hands Center (Open-Ended Activity)

Content area: Teacher's choice

Skills: Fine-motor coordination, teacher's choice

Activities:

1. Make a jeans envelope.
2. Make a "hands" game.

Measure Me Neat Center

Content areas: Science, math

Skills: Linear measurement, communicating

Activities:

1. Trace your hands and feet.
2. Draw and measure lines. Record their measurements.
3. Measure "things that make me neat." Record measurements on the student activity page.

TEACHER'S DIRECTIONS FOR THE ALL ABOUT US CENTER

Content areas: Reading, handwriting

Skills: Fine-motor coordination, communicating

Materials needed:

Bulletin board
Student activity patterns
Paper (wallpaper, notebook, handwriting, construction)
Pencil
Crayons
Stapler and staples
Scissors
Thumbtacks
Teacher-made books
Metric scale and meterstick (optional)

Materials preparation:

1. Prepare the bulletin board as shown here. Student books will be tacked to the bulletin board upon completion. Students may read the displayed books at a prearranged time.

2. Make two riddle books using student activity patterns. The books are designed with one or two sentences and illustrations per page. The emphasis is on self-concept. Some examples are:

I weigh _____ kilograms.

I am _____ centimeters tall.

I have _____ hair and _____ eyes.

I live at _____.

I like to play _____.

I like to eat _____.

My favorite restaurant is _____.

At school, I like _____.

At home, I help by _____.

I have _____ pets.

I am happy when _____.

I wish _____.

My name is _____.

The student writes his or her name on the last page. The other students are encouraged to read the entire book to guess who the book is about.

3. In preparing the books, you need to determine

    a. The number of pages in the book (older students can do several).

    b. The type of paper you will use for the cover and content pages.

    c. How to assemble the book.

      • Older students may trace the student activity pattern for the cover and content pages, staple the book together at the top, write the book, and illustrate it (referring to the teacher's book).

      • You may prefer to staple a book together yourself for younger students, (ditto the student activity pattern pages with one open-ended sentence written on each page). The students may write a few words to complete the sentence (you or an aide may help students with words at a prearranged time). Students can then illustrate and cut out the pages.

Directions for file folder activities:

Activity 1

The student assembles his or her book according to the book directions.

Activity 2

The student writes and illustrates the pages.

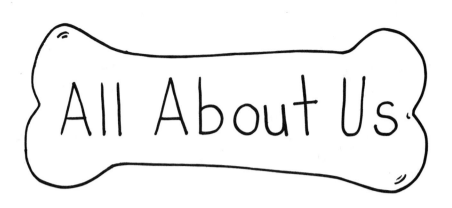

All About Us

1 Make your book.

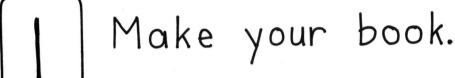

2 Copy words onto each page. Color each page.

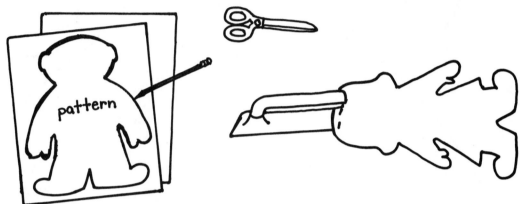

**Student
Activity
Pattern**

**Student
Activity
Pattern**

TEACHER'S DIRECTIONS FOR THE MY BODY CENTER

Content areas: Reading, art, handwriting

Skills: Fine-motor coordination, using reference materials, creating

Materials needed:

A roll of 30-inch-wide white paper

Two paper clips per student

Box for paper

Masking tape

Pencil

Crayons

Body parts references (chart, dictionary, pictionary)

Materials preparation:

Cut strips of 30-inch-wide paper, one for each student. (Cut the paper a few inches longer than the height of the tallest student in your class.) It is helpful to roll, paper clip, and stand the paper in a box at this center.

Directions for file folder activities:

Activity 1

The student gets a friend to help tape the four corners of the paper to the floor. The student removes his or her shoes and lies down on the paper, enabling the friend to trace around him or her with a pencil.

Activity 2

The student looks up the body parts in the reference and labels them. He or she may color the clothes, hair, eyes, and so on. The student removes the tape and rolls up the paper. He or she tapes the paper and writes his or her name on the outside of it.

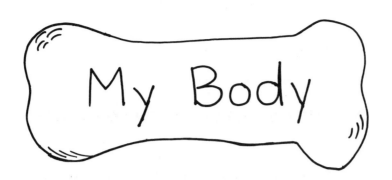

My Body

1 Get a friend to trace around your body.

2 Write on the parts of your body. Then you may color it.

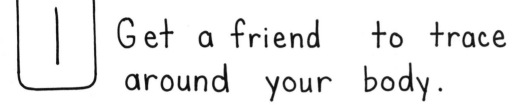

head
hair
shoulder
arm
eye
nose
mouth
chin
neck

File Folder Directions

121

TEACHER'S DIRECTIONS FOR THE HEART CENTER

Content areas: Reading, science, math

Skills: Listening, measuring time, communicating

Materials needed:

Copies of student activity page

Stethoscope

Rubbing alcohol in a small jar with a lid

Cotton balls

Electric clock with a minute hand

Pencil

Tape recorder

Cassette tape

A book about the heart such as *Hear Your Heart*, by Paul Showers, Thomas Y. Crowell Co., New York, 1968.

Materials preparation:

1. Prepare a cassette tape of the book and the following directions for the student activity page:
   a. Write your name on the ditto.
   b. Clean the stethoscope's ear plugs with cotton and alcohol.
   c. Put on the stethoscope and listen to your heart.
   d. Look at the minute hand on the clock. Begin to count your heartbeats when the minute hand is on 12. Stop when the hand reaches 12 again.
   e. Write down the number of beats for the resting rate on the ditto.
2. Count and record your heart rate after walking and running. (You may prefer to cue the 60-second timing rates on the cassette tape using "Ready, listen, go . . . stop.")

Directions for file folder activities:

Activity 1

The student listens to the cassette tape of the book.

Activity 2

The student follows the tape-recorded directions to measure his or her heartbeats. The student records his or her heartbeats on the student activity page. (Students may work in pairs at this center, with one student acting as a timer for the other student.)

Heart

1 Listen to the book.

2 Do ditto.

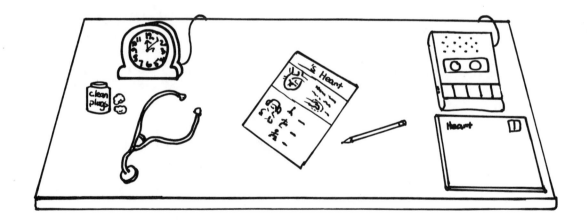

_____'s Heart

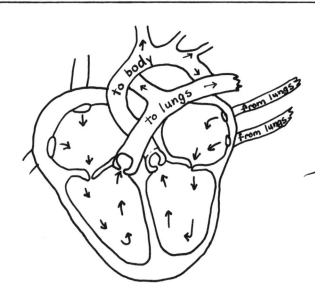

My heart is about this big.

My fist.

Resting

_____ beats a minute

Walking

_____ beats a minute

Running

_____ beats a minute

Student Activity Page

124

TEACHER'S DIRECTIONS FOR THE TEETH CENTER

Content areas: Science, art, handwriting

Skills: Observing, creating, fine-motor coordination

Materials needed:

One plaque-disclosing tablet per student

Mirror

Paper

Handwriting paper

Crayons, marking pens, or colored pencils

Paste

Scissors

An assortment of 3-by-6-inch construction paper

Student activity pattern

Teacher-made example of rules

Materials preparation:

Handwrite several rules, such as

1. Brush teeth after meals.
2. Don't eat foods containing a lot of sugar.
3. See the dentist two times a year.

Directions for file folder activities:

Activity 1

The student chews the plaque-disclosing tablet and looks at his or her teeth in the mirror. (The teeth will look spotted because the dye in the tablet sticks to the plaque.) The student may then rinse with water.

Activity 2

1. The student draws his or her head on paper with crayons, marking pens, or colored pencils.
2. The student may make a construction-paper toothbrush or trace, color, and cut out the following pattern.

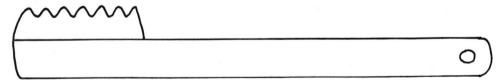

3. The student pastes the toothbrush onto the picture of the head.

Activity 3

The student writes several rules on handwriting paper. (Younger students may copy the teacher-made example of the three rules. Older students may write three or more original rules.)

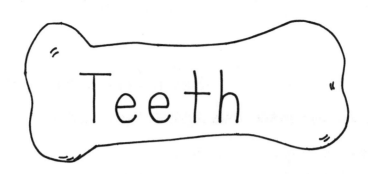

Teeth

1 How well did you brush your teeth today? Chew one tablet. Look in the mirror.

2 Draw your head. Don't forget a smile. Paste on a toothbrush.

name

3 Write the rules for healthy teeth.

1. Brush

File Folder Directions

TEACHER'S DIRECTIONS FOR THE SKIN CENTER

Content areas: Science, art

Skills: Observing, creating

Materials needed:

Magnifying glass

Red ink stamp pad

Three fine-line marking pens in dark colors

Paper squares, 6 inches or larger

Stapler, staples, paste, large construction paper (optional)

Materials preparation:

1. Cover the work table with paper or plastic.
2. Determine
   a. The number of pieces of paper needed for each student.
   b. How to assemble the finished pictures (that is, staple them into a book, paste them on construction paper, and so on).

Directions for file folder activities:

Activity 1

The student uses a magnifying glass to look at his or her arm (skin and hair), hands, fingernails, any scars, and so on. Then the student examines his or her fingertips for loops and lines.

Activity 2

1. The student uses his or her thumb, ink stamp pad, and paper to make thumbprint pictures.
2. The student adds details with marking pens (referring to file folder direction examples).
3. Then the student assembles the pictures according to your directions.

Optional Activities

1. Older students may label thumbprint pictures and write adverbial phrases, such as "a cat by a bowl of milk," "a bird in a tree," "a turtle by a rock."
2. Students may use thumbprints to decorate wrapping paper, patches for T-shirts, stationery, or greeting cards.

Skin

1 Look at your skin.

fingernail

arm

hair

Can you find loops and lines on your fingertips?

2 Make thumbprint pictures.

stamp pad

markers

File Folder Directions

128

TEACHER'S DIRECTIONS FOR THE BONES CENTER

Content areas: Science, handwriting, art

Skills: Observing, creating, fine-motor coordination

Materials needed:

Collection of chicken, beef, ham, and fish bones

Magnifying glass

Overhead projector and screen

Marking pen for overhead transparency

Scissors

Pencil

Crayons

Paste

Black and white construction paper

Copies of student activity page

Teacher-made transparency of student activity page

Materials preparation:

1. Make a transparency of the student activity page on an acetate sheet to use on an overhead projector.
2. If an overhead projector is unavailable,
   a. Ditto copies of the student activity page for the student to use in Activity 2.
   b. Attach a skeleton chart to a chalkboard. The student writes the name of the bones using the student activity page as a reference.

Directions for file folder activities:

Activity 1

The student observes various bones with a magnifying glass. (Encourage students to compare their own bones with similar animal bones, such as a chicken leg with their leg.)

Activity 2

The student writes the names of the bones on the overhead projector transparency with a marking pen.

Activity 3

The student draws a skeleton on white paper with a pencil. Then he or she cuts and pastes the skeleton onto black paper.

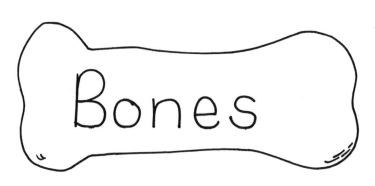

Bones

1 Look at the bones.

2 Write the names of the bones.

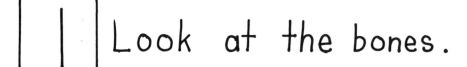

3 Make a skeleton on white paper.
Paste it onto black paper.

File Folder Directions

130

Bones

collarbone

skull

jaw

humerus

ribs

spine

hip bone

femur

knee cap

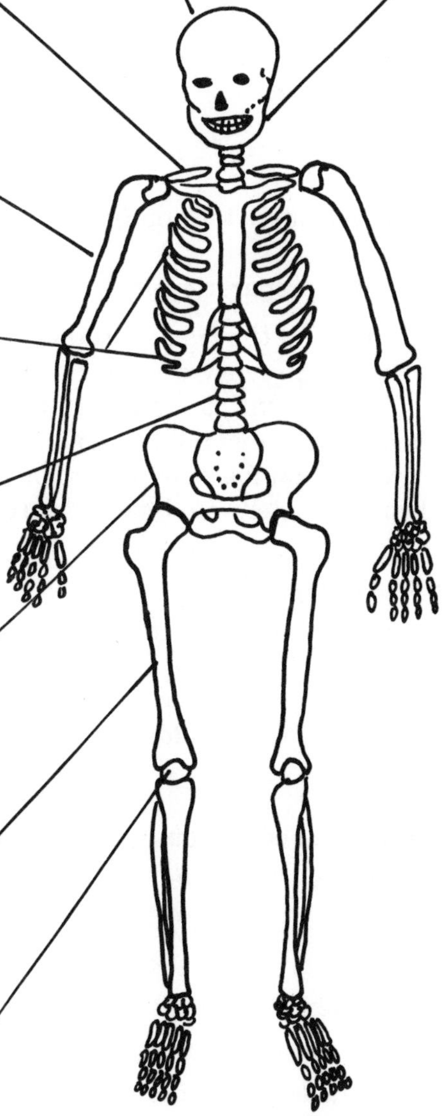

(your name)

TEACHER'S DIRECTIONS FOR THE HANDS CENTER

Content area: Teacher's choice

Skills: Fine-motor coordination, teacher's choice

Materials needed:

Copies of the student activity pages

Teacher-made "hands" game

Teacher-made jeans envelope

Pencil

Paste

Crayons

Scissors

Reference chart for younger students (optional)

Materials preparation:

1. Use a copy of the Hands student activity page to make a matching game to reinforce or review a skill. Some ideas are antonyms, contractions, math problems, counting by fives (write number word on matching hand), and money (write amount on hand and student traces coins on matching hand). Write the numbers or words on the heel of the hands to insure visibility when the fingers are inserted into the Jeans pockets.

2. Make a Jeans envelope for the game using a copy of the Jeans student activity page.

3. Optional: Make a reference chart for the students by writing words or problems on a copy of the Hands student activity page.

Directions for file folder activities:

Activity 1

The student colors, cuts pocket slits, folds, and pastes the sides of the Jeans student activity page to form an envelope. The student writes his or her name in the blank.

Activity 2

1. The student copies the "hands" game on a Hands student activity page.

2. The student completes the work.

3. The student colors and cuts out the hands.

4. The student can play the game (alone or with a friend) by placing the matching hands into the Jeans pockets. (Older students may want to make eight sets of matching hands by using two Hands student activity pages.)

Hands

1 Make the jeans.

fold ↗

2 Make the hand game.

 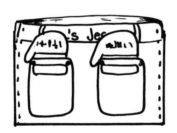 

File Folder Directions

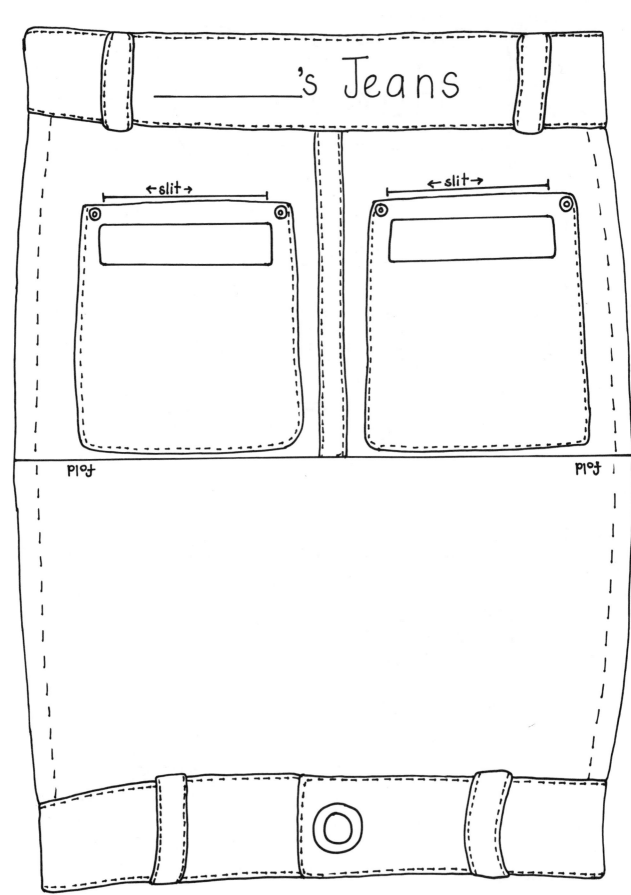

_____'s Jeans

←slit→   ←slit→

fold   fold

Student Activity Page

Student Activity Page

TEACHER'S DIRECTIONS FOR THE MEASURE ME NEAT CENTER

Content areas: Science, math

Skills: Linear measurement, communicating

Materials needed:

24-by-24-inch paper

Meterstick or yardstick

Marking pens

Pencil

Crayons

Copies of student activity page

Box containing soap, towel, washcloth, toothbrush, comb, toothpaste, shampoo, and brush

Teacher-made example paper

Materials preparation:

1. To make the example paper, trace around hands and bare feet with a black marking pen or pencil. Use a red marking pen and a meterstick or yardstick to draw a line to connect the hands. Use a blue marking pen to draw a line to connect the feet. Use a green marking pen to draw a line across the width of one hand and one foot.

2. Additional lines may be drawn for the older student to measure, such as a line connecting the right hand and right foot or the left and right foot, or they can measure the length of ring finger, and the length of little finger.

3. You may prefer to give older students written directions, such as "Use an orange pen to connect your right hand and right foot."

Directions for file folder activities:

Activity 1

1. The student traces his or her hands and bare feet with a pencil or crayon on large paper (on the floor).

2. The student uses marking pens and a meterstick or yardstick to draw and measure lines according to your example.

3. The student writes the measurements on the lines.

Activity 2

The student uses a meterstick or yardstick to measure the objects in the box. He or she records the measurements on the student activity page. Coloring the page is optional.

Measure Me Neat

1 Trace your hands and feet.

Make lines.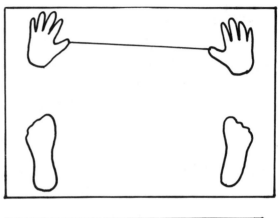

Measure the lines.

Write answers on the lines.

2 Measure the things that keep you neat. Write the answers on the ditto.

Things that make me neat.

File Folder Directions

Measure Me Neat

SOAP

soap _____

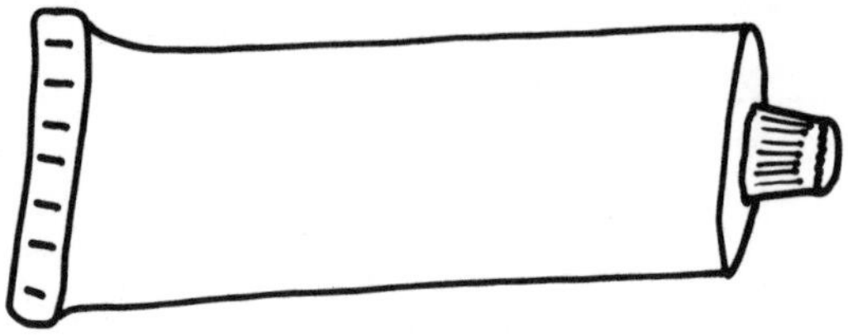

toothpaste _____

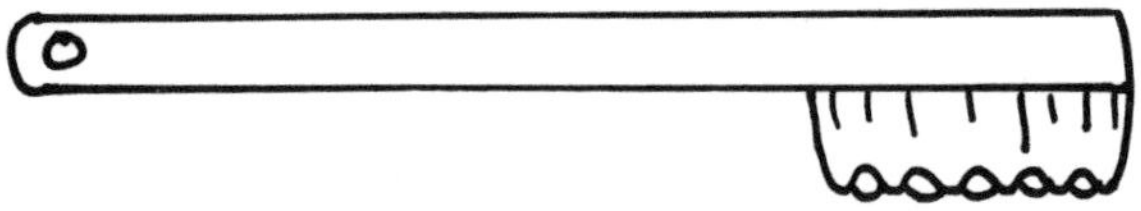

toothbrush _____

shampoo _____

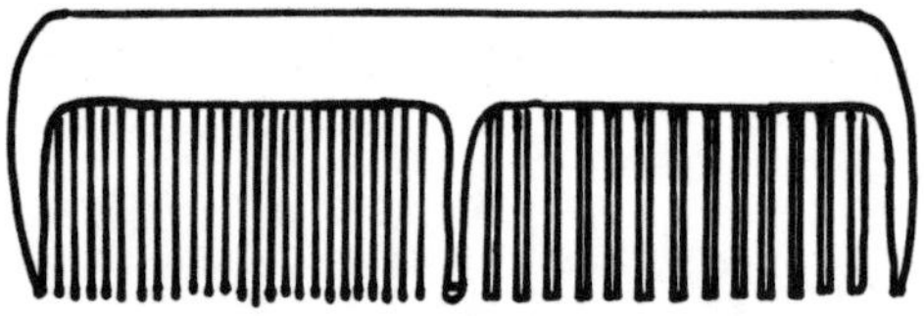

comb _____

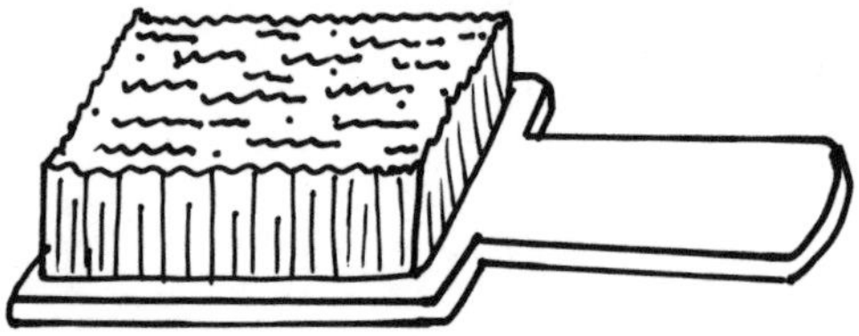

brush _____

washcloth _____

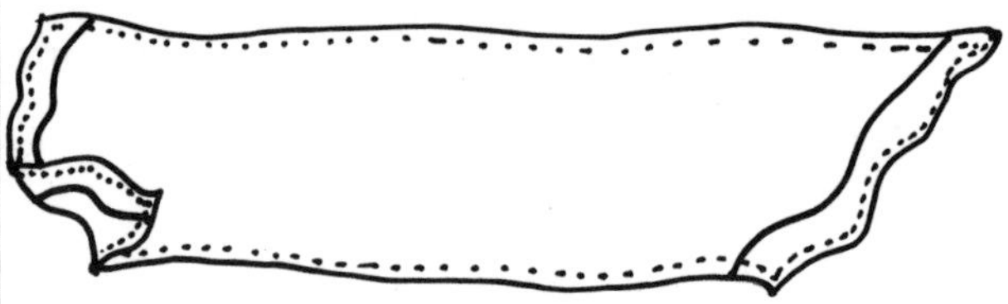

towel _____

Name _____

Student Activity Page

138

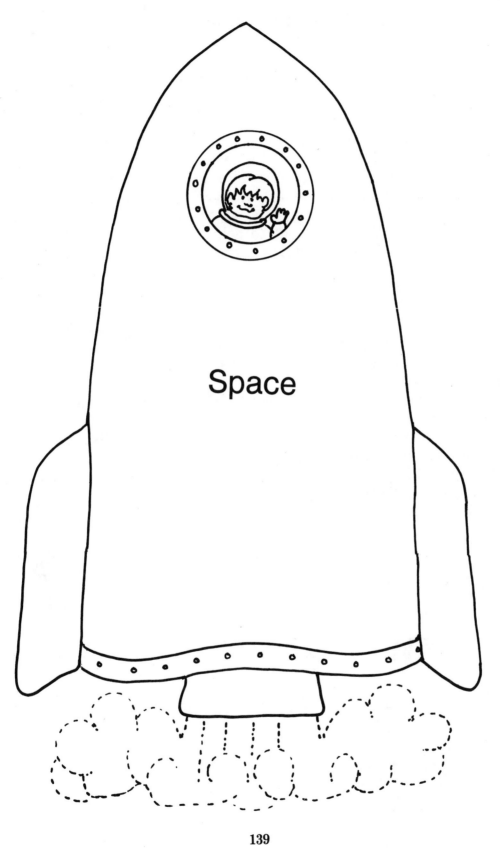

Space

139

BLAST OFF!

Date _____

Dear Parent,

We will begin working in learning centers about space next week. We will study the solar system, constellations, astronauts, and gravity.

Encourage your child to contribute newspaper and magazine articles pertaining to current space travel events for class discussions.

Your child will need an empty potato chip can with a lid or a similar container (approximately 8½ by 3 inches) to make a telescope at the Constellation Center. You may want to help your child learn to recognize some of the common constellations (for example, the Big Dipper and the Little Dipper) in the night sky. You may also help him or her develop an awareness of the phases of the moon, which will be emphasized at the Moon Center.

At the Astronaut Center your child will create a space vehicle. Please help all of our "inventors" by sending unwanted items (egg cartons, cardboard toweling or wrapping paper tubes, produce trays, and boxes) for this center.

Matching planet riddles to pictures of planets on the bulletin board will be the main activity of the Solar System Center.

Map skills will be used at the Earth Center. Various locations will be identified by your child on a globe.

Telling time will be the math skill featured at the Astronaut's Day Center, where your child will create a digital clock.

Thank you very much for your continued support.

Sincerely,

_____
Your child's teacher

GROUP ACTIVITIES

A field trip to a planetarium or a space museum is an excellent group activity.

Putting on your own constellation show is an optional group activity. You will need to collect several overexposed (black) negatives of 35mm film. Prepare the negatives in the following way. Use a straight pin to poke holes resembling a different constellation in each negative. Place the negatives in a projector for group viewing on a screen.

You may want to use the following books in preparing the constellation group activity:

Branley, Franklyn, *The Big Dipper*, Thomas Y. Crowell Co., New York, 1962.

Branley, Franklyn, *The Sky Is Full of Stars*, Thomas Y. Crowell Co., New York, 1981.

Reed, W. Maxwell, *Patterns in the Sky*, William Morrow and Co., New York, 1951.

Rey, H. A., *Find the Constellations*, Houghton-Mifflin Co., New York, 1966.

Follow-up group activities can include group discussions and creative writing about constellations and zodiac signs. Your students might want to make a graph of their zodiac signs.

BOARDWORK ACTIVITIES

1. Make fact cards about the sun, moon, and planets.

2. Create picture-word reference charts of the solar system. List the names of the planets, moon, and sun on the board in a scrambled order. The student unscrambles the words, writes them down, and illustrates them in an eight-box format. Examples are nuS (Sun), sraM (Mars), rEtha (Earth), seuVn (Venus).

3. Develop creative writing activities, such as:

   "If I went to the moon, I would (explore, see, and so on) . . ."
   "My dog was a stowaway on a spaceship."
   "An astronaut got the hiccups and . . ."
   "If I went on a space mission, I would take a backpack. In my backpack I would carry . . ."

4. Write the word "astronaut" on the chalkboard. The student makes a list of all the words he or she can find in the word. Some words to find are: star, ran, tan, rust, run, sun, son, ton, tar, trot, not, rut, nut, and strut. An older student might find four or more of these words in a dictionary and write their definitions. A younger student can use two or more words in sentences and illustrate them. For example, "I see the sun." "I can run fast."

5. List days of the week and their Roman names in a column format or an eight-box format (the student's name could be written in the eighth box). For example, Sunday, Sol (sun); Monday, Luna (moon); Tuesday, Mars; Wednesday, Mercury; Thursday, Jupiter; Friday, Venus; and Saturday, Saturn. The student can illustrate his or her favorite activity (television program, reading, chores) for each day.

   A good book to establish calendar background information is Evenson, A.E., *About the History of the Calendar*, Children's Press, Chicago, 1972.

6. Make a time–space capsule envelope (two pieces of 12-by-18-inch construction paper stapled together) or shoe box. On the outside write,

   "_____'s time space capsule.
                     child's name

   Do not open until _____."
                                        date

   Inside the time–space capsule include lists or pictures of your favorite TV show, favorite book, best friends, best sporting event, favorite comic strip, favorite clothes, and so on.

7. Make an "outer space" puppet using a variety of materials, then write a story about it. "My friend the Martian likes _____."

8. Create time books:
   - An older student copies sentences from the board onto blank pieces of paper, completes the sentences, illustrates pages, and staples them into a book. He or she may draw a clock on each page.

     "I get up at _____."
     "I eat breakfast at _____."
     "I go to school at _____."
     "I go to recess at _____."
     "I eat lunch at _____."
     "I go home at _____."
     "I eat supper at _____."

   - A younger student may do similar work with fewer pages in a book stapled together by the teacher.

9. Write experience stories following group activities.

SPACE CENTER MARKER

Distribute copies of the spaceship marker to the students. The students can cut out their markers and place them near the Space Learning Centers.

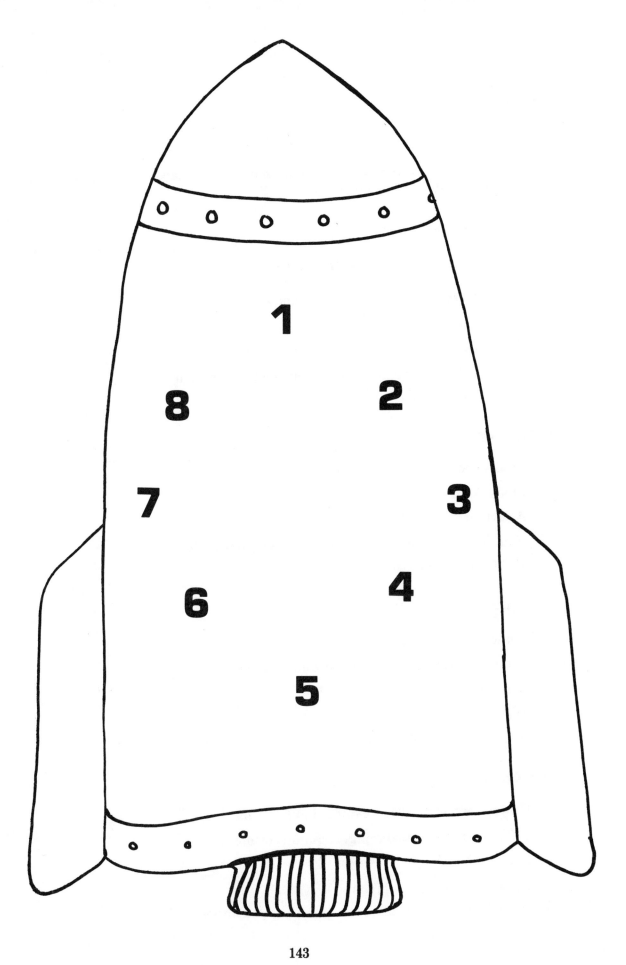

LEARNING CENTERS LIST

These learning centers relate to various aspects of space, including the solar system, astronauts, and gravity.

Solar System Center

(A bulletin board is used with this center.)

Content areas: Science, reading, handwriting

Skills: Matching, communicating

Activities:

1. Match riddles to planet pictures on the bulletin board.
2. Write planet names and riddles.

Earth Center

Content areas: Geography, art

Skills: Map-reading, creating

Activities:

1. Find the globe locations listed on the student activity page.
2. Paint a picture of the Earth.

Sun Center

Content areas: Art, math

Skills: Creating, fine-motor coordination, linear measurement

Activities:

1. Make a sun.
2. Tie stars to the sun.

Moon Center

Content areas: Science, reading, handwriting

Skills: Matching, predicting, communicating

Activities:

1. Draw the Man in the Moon.
2. Write "I think _____" sentences about the Moon.

Constellations Center

Content area: Science

Skills: Observing, fine-motor coordination

Activities:

1. Make constellation pin designs.
2. Make a telescope for viewing the constellations.

Gravity Center

Content areas: Science, reading

Skills: Observing, listening, predicting

Activities:

1. Listen to a story about gravity and do experiments.
2. Make a parachute.

Astronaut Center

Content areas: Handwriting, art

Skills: Creating, creative writing

Activities:

1. Invent a vehicle for space travel.
2. Write a creative story: "If I were an astronaut . . ."

Time Center (Open-Ended Activity)

Content area: Math

Skills: Measuring time, fine-motor coordination

Activities:

1. Complete the time skill on the student activity page.
2. Make a digital clock.

TEACHER'S DIRECTIONS FOR THE SOLAR SYSTEM CENTER

Content areas: Science, reading, handwriting

Skills: Matching, communicating

Materials needed:

Bulletin board

Planet riddle cards and container

Thumbtacks and container

Crayons

Pencil

Copies of student activity page

Materials preparation:

1. Make "The Solar System" bulletin board as shown on the file folder directions page.

2. Make nine planet riddle cards, as described here:

   a. Use 3-by-5-inch index cards. Make the activity self-checking by writing the planet number on the back of each card (note that the planets are numbered on the student activity page).

   b. Some ideas for "What planet am I?" riddles are:

   - I am the smallest planet. I am nearest the Sun. What planet am I? (Mercury—1)

   - I am the hottest planet. I am about the same size as Earth. What planet am I? (Venus—2)

   - I am covered with plants and animals. I am 93 million miles from the sun. What planet am I? (Earth—3)

   - I am called the Red Planet. I am made of red rocks. What planet am I? (Mars—4)

   - I am the largest planet. I have a Giant Red Spot. What planet am I? (Jupiter—5)

   - I have rings around me. I am made of chemicals lighter than water. What planet am I? (Saturn—6)

   - I spin in a strange way. I seem to be lying down while the other planets stand up. What planet am I? (Uranus—7)

   - I am greenish blue. I am a giant gas planet. What planet am I? (Neptune—8)

   - I am the coldest planet. I am farthest from the sun. What planet am I? (Pluto—9)

Directions for file folder activities:

Activity 1

The student tacks riddle cards under the matching planet names on the bulletin board.

Activity 2

The younger student writes the names of the planets in their order from the sun on the student activity page.

The older student writes the planet names and the riddles on the student activity page. Students may color the pictures.

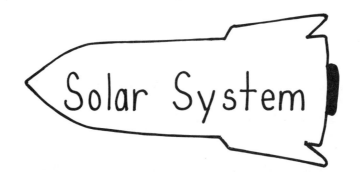

Solar System

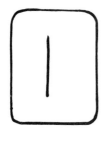

1

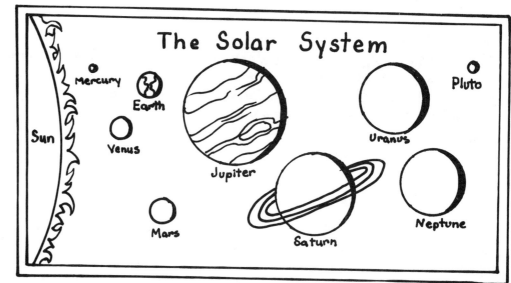

Planet
Riddles

Match the riddles to the planets.

2

Do the ditto.

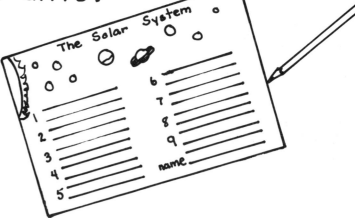

The Solar System

Sun

Mercury

Venus

Earth

Mars

Jupiter

Saturn

Uranus

Neptune

Pluto

1

2

3

4

5

6

7

8

9

Name

Student Activity Page

149

TEACHER'S DIRECTIONS FOR THE EARTH CENTER

Content areas: Geography, art

Skills: Map-reading, creating

Materials needed:

Globe of the Earth

Copies of student activity page

Pencil

Crayons

Paint

Paintbrushes

Paper

Easel

Ten pieces of construction paper in assorted colors
   (approximately 1½-inch squares)

Materials preparation:

1. Cut 10 different shapes (circle, semicircle, triangle, square, rectangle, octagon, trapezoid, pentagon, cone, and an outline of your state) out of construction paper.

2. Attach the 10 shapes with masking tape to a globe at the locations listed on the student activity page.

Directions for file folder activities:

Activity 1

The student uses the globe to find the places listed on the student activity page. He or she draws the corresponding shape for each location on the activity page.

Activity 2

The student paints a picture of the Earth.

Earth

1 Do ditto with the globe.

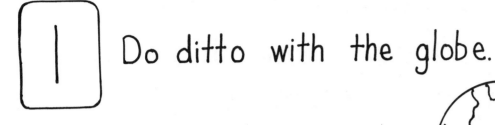

2 Paint a picture
of Earth.

File Folder Directions

Earth

Use the globe to find these places. Draw the shape you found at each place on the globe.

_____ 1. Canada

_____ 2. North Pole

_____ 3. South Pole

_____ 4. Ocean

_____ 5. Equator

_____ 6. United States

_____ 7. Our State

_____ 8. Alaska

_____ 9. Hawaii

_____ 10. Australia

Name _____

TEACHER'S DIRECTIONS FOR THE SUN CENTER

Content areas: Art, math

Skills: Linear measurement, creating, fine-motor coordination

Materials needed:

Copies of student activity page

Teacher-made sun pattern

One 9-inch paper plate per student

Ruler

Paper puncher

Scissors

Crayons

Pencil

One 7-foot-long piece of yarn or string per student

Materials preparation:

To make the sun pattern, color a paper plate and cut it into a seven-pointed star shape, as pictured in the file folder directions. Punch a hole at each point with a paper puncher.

Directions for file folder activities:

Activity 1

1. The student makes the sun, referring to the teacher-made sun pattern.
2. He or she draws a face on the plate.
3. The student colors and cuts out the stars on the student activity page. He or she punches a hole in the dot on each star.

Activity 2

1. The student measures and cuts the yarn into seven pieces, each 12 inches long.
2. He or she ties one end of each piece of yarn through the hole in the star.
3. He or she ties the opposite end of the yarn to a hole in the sun. The yarn in the top point of the sun may be formed into a loop hanger.

Optional Activity

An older student may write additional sun facts on the back of each star by using various reference materials.

Sun

1

Make a Sun.

plate

pattern

Punch holes in each point.

2

Tie the stars to the Sun.

string

File Folder Directions

154

Color these and cut them out.
Punch a hole at each dot.

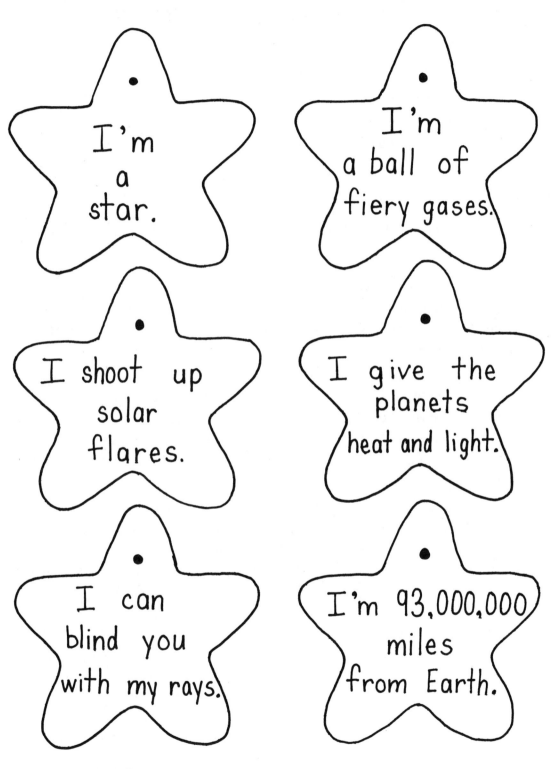

I'm
a
star.

I'm
a ball of
fiery gases.

I shoot up
solar
flares.

I give the
planets
heat and light.

I can
blind you
with my rays.

I'm 93,000,000
miles
from Earth.

Student Activity Page

TEACHER'S DIRECTIONS FOR THE MOON CENTER

Content areas: Science, reading, handwriting

Skills: Matching, predicting, communicating

Materials needed:

Copies of student activity page

Teacher-made moon sentence-starter strips

Scissors

Pencil

Crayons

2-by-11-inch construction-paper strips

Container for construction-paper strips

Materials preparation:

1. To make the moon sentence-starter strips, write sentence starters about the moon on different colors of construction-paper strips. Some ideas are

   I think the moon is made of _____.

   I think _____ live on the moon.

   I think the footprints on the moon were made by _____.

   I think the weather on the moon is _____.

   I think the moon is _____ miles from the Earth.

   I think I would weigh _____ on the moon.

   I think astronauts rode on the moon in a _____.

   I think the astronauts found _____ on the moon.

2. Display the sentence starter strips at the center on the bulletin board or divider, or in envelopes, coffee cans, or other containers.

3. Provide strips of corresponding colors of construction paper for the students.

4. Provide a container for the students to place their completed sentence strips in.

Directions for file folder activities:

Activity 1

1. The student colors and cuts slits in the Man in the Moon student activity page.

2. He or she cuts apart the moon picture and word strips at the bottom of the student activity page.

3. He or she inserts the strips into the slits on the Man in the Moon to match the moon picture with the word.

Activity 2

The student copies and completes a moon sentence strip on a corresponding color of paper. The student writes his or her name on the back of the paper and places it in the appropriate container. (You will determine the required number of strips for your students.)

Follow-up Activities

On the final day of the Space Centers, you can read and discuss the sentence strips, discuss facts about the moon, and make a vocabulary chart that the students may use for creative writing.

Moon

1 Make the Man in the Moon.

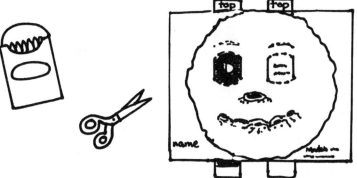

2 Write I think... about the moon.

File Folder Directions

Man in the Moon

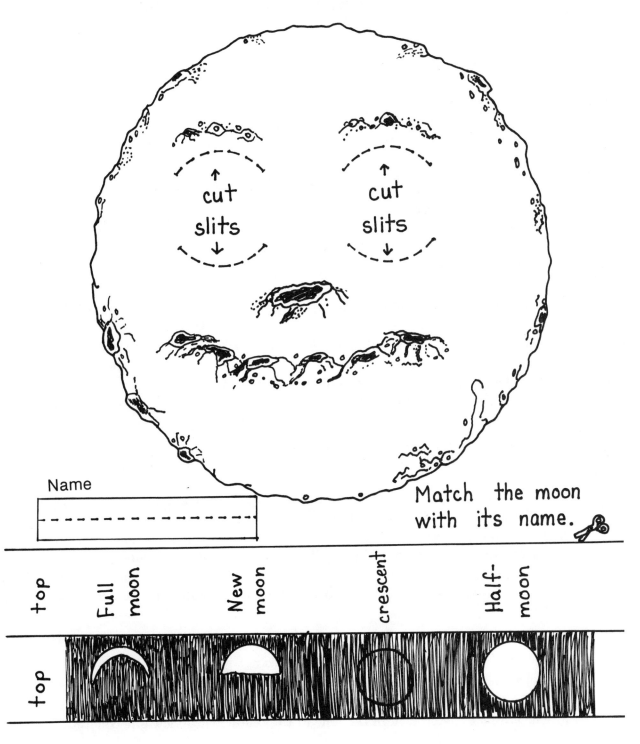

cut
slits

cut
slits

Name

Match the moon
with its name.

top

Full
moon

New
moon

crescent

Half-
moon

top

Student Activity Page

TEACHER'S DIRECTIONS FOR THE CONSTELLATIONS CENTER

Content area: Science

Skills: Observing, fine-motor coordination

Materials needed:

Copies of student activity pages

One potato chip can with lid or similar container, (approximately 8½ by 3 inches) per student

Teacher-made telescope

Hammer

Nail

White crayon

Scissors

Straight pins

Stapler and staples

Carpet sample

9-by-12-inch black construction paper

Materials preparation:

1. To make a telescope, make a hole in the center of the metal end of the potato chip can with a hammer and a nail. Leave the lid on the opposite end of the can.

2. Prepare the student activity page for a pin design. Ditto the student activity page and staple its top corners to the black construction paper. Put a straight pin in the top of the student activity page.

3. Provide a carpet sample at the learning center to protect the desk top from pin scratches when the student makes the pin design.

Directions for file folder activities:

Activity 1

1. The student uses the pin to poke holes through the circle outlines of the constellations on the student activity page.

2. He or she removes the student activity page from the black construction paper (the constellation designs will be visible on the black paper).

3. He or she uses a white crayon to connect the dots in each circle on the black paper (similar to dot-to-dot pictures). The student cuts out the six black circles.

Activity 2

1. The student makes a telescope referring to the teacher-made example.

2. He or she places one black constellation circle at a time inside the lid of the telescope and puts the lid back on the telescope.

3. The student looks through the hole of the telescope to view one constellation at a time.

Optional Activity

The student may cover the outside of the can with paper, self-stick vinyl, or other material.

Constellations

1 Do a pin design of the constellations.

With a white crayon, connect the pin holes on the black circles. Cut out the black circles.

2 Now look at your constellations through your can.

black circle in lid →

Constellations

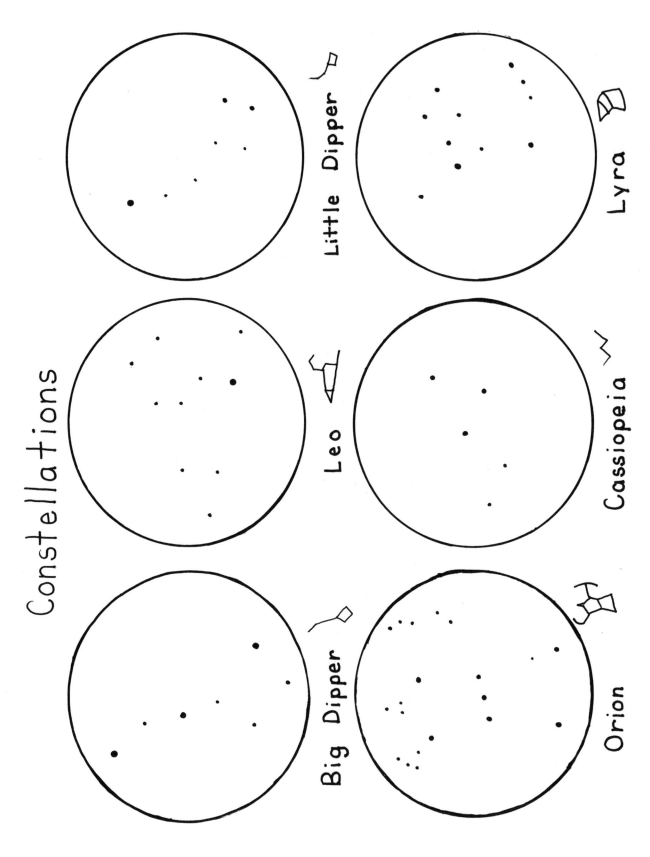

Little Dipper

Lyra

Leo

Cassiopeia

Big Dipper

Orion

Student Activity Page

162

TEACHER'S DIRECTIONS FOR THE GRAVITY CENTER

Content areas: Science, reading

Skills: Observing, listening, predicting

Materials needed:

Masking tape	Scissors
One 64-inch piece of string per student	Meterstick or yardstick
One ⅜-inch washer per student	Tape recorder
One 14-inch-square piece of plastic per student	Cassette tape

A book about gravity, such as Branley, Franklyn, *Gravity Is a Mystery*, Thomas Y. Crowell Co., New York, 1970; Lefkowitz, R. J., *Forces in the Earth*, Parents Magazine Press, New York, 1942; Ridiman, Bob, *What Is a Shadow?*, Parents Magazine Press, New York, 1973.

Materials preparation:

1. Prepare a cassette tape of the book. You may also want to tape directions enabling the student to perform simple air and gravity experiments described in the book.

2. In addition, you may want to discuss or display pictures of astronauts living in gravity-free conditions (walking, eating, sleeping, bathing, and maneuvering outside the spacecraft) at this center.

Directions for file folder activities:

Activity 1

The student listens to the cassette tape of the book. Optional: The student performs simple air and gravity experiments according to your directions. The three books listed under "materials needed" may be used as resources. Additional books about air and gravity experiments are

Habben, Dorothy, *Science Experiments That Really Work*, Follett Publishing Co., Chicago, 1970.

Milgrom, Harry, *First Experiments with Gravity*, E. P. Dutton and Co., Inc., New York, 1966.

Pine, Tillie S. and Levine, Joseph, *Air All Around*, Whittlesey House, McGraw-Hill Book Co., New York, 1960.

Ridiman, Bob, *Simple Science Fun*, Parents Magazine Press, New York, 1972.

Activity 2

The student makes a parachute by measuring and cutting the string into four 16-inch pieces. He or she then tapes one end of each string to the corners of a piece of plastic and ties the opposite end of each string to a washer.

Follow-Up Group Outdoor Activity

The students sit in one line on a playground. You or a student then conduct the following gravity demonstration:

1. Hold a washer in one hand and a student's parachute in the other hand.
2. Throw both objects in the air at the same time.
3. Have students observe the descending objects.
4. Discuss the following questions:
   a. What pulls the objects down to the ground? (gravity pulls all objects the same way to Earth regardless of their size)
   b. Which object landed first? (the washer)
   c. Why did the parachute descend at a slower rate? (the air pushed up against it)
   d. What would happen if you tried this experiment on the moon? (both objects would hit the ground at the same time) Why? (there is no air on the moon)

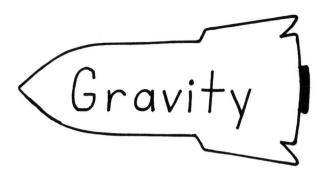

Gravity

1 Listen to the book about gravity.

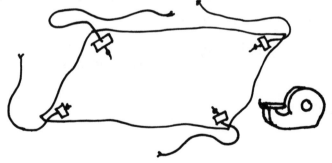

2 Make a parachute.

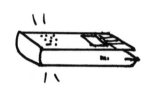

Cut string

Tape on string.

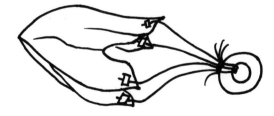

Tie to a weight.

File Folder Directions

TEACHER'S DIRECTIONS FOR THE ASTRONAUT CENTER

Content areas: Handwriting, art

Skills: Creating, creative writing

Materials needed:

A collection of junk materials, such as cardboard tubes, boxes of various sizes, plastic bottles, lids, spools, foam trays from meat or produce, straws, cardboard strips, assorted colors and sizes of construction paper.

Copies of student activity page

Pencil

Crayons

Scissors

Glue

Masking tape

Materials preparation:

Use books, audiovisual aids, and so on to establish background information about astronauts and space inventions (for example, the moon buggy and the robot).

Directions for file folder activities:

Activity 1

The student uses the junk materials to invent a vehicle for space travel.

Activity 2

The student writes a creative story on the student activity page using space vocabulary. He or she illustrates the story on the back of the student activity page.

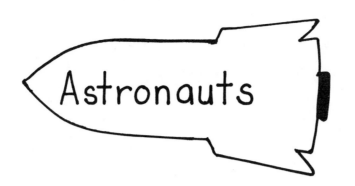

Astronauts

1 Invent a vehicle for space travel.

?

2 Do ditto.

File Folder Directions

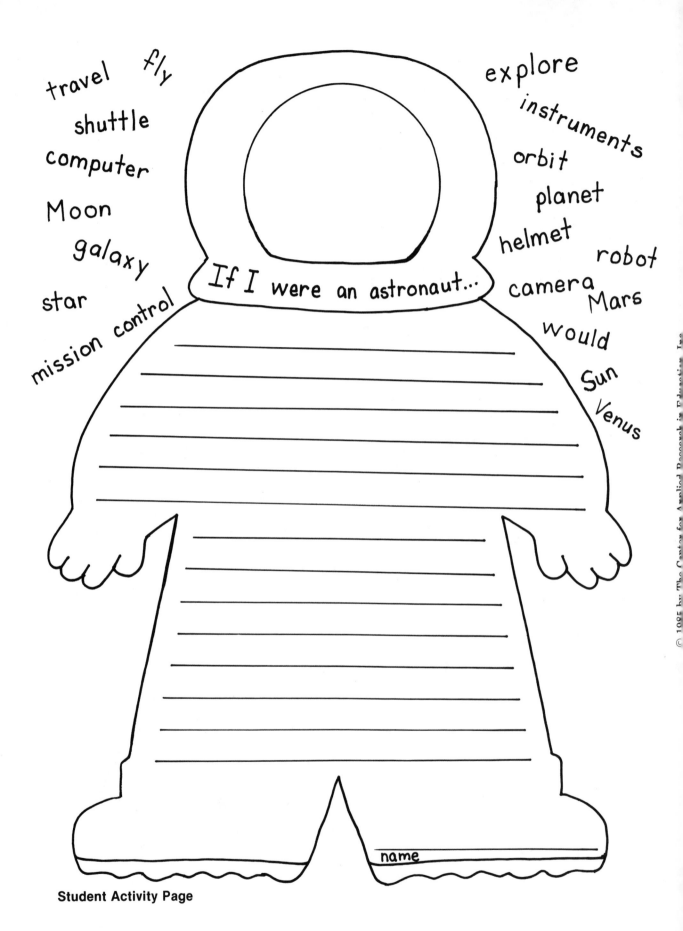

travel fly

shuttle

computer

Moon

galaxy

star

mission control

explore

instruments

orbit

planet

helmet

robot

camera Mars

would

Sun

Venus

If I were an astronaut...

name

Student Activity Page

TEACHER'S DIRECTIONS FOR THE TIME CENTER

Content area: Math

Skills: Measuring time, fine-motor coordination

Materials needed:

Copies of student activity pages

Scissors

Pencil

Crayons

Paste

Materials preparation:

1. Determine the time skill (for example, timing to the hour, half-hour, or quarter-hour) to be reinforced or reviewed by the students.
2. Fill in times on Astronaut's Day student activity page before dittoing it. The student draws the hands on the clock to show the corresponding time.

Directions for file folder activities:

Activity 1

The student completes the appropriate time skill on the Astronaut's Day student activity page and colors the pictures.

Activity 2

1. The student writes his or her name and colors and cuts slits in the digital clock on the Student's Clock activity page.
2. The student cuts apart the number strips and inserts them into the corresponding slits on the clock.
3. He or she pastes the ends of each strip to form a loop.

Optional Activity

The student may use the clock to duplicate each time listed on the Astronaut's Day student activity page.

Time

1 Do the ditto.

2 Make the clock.

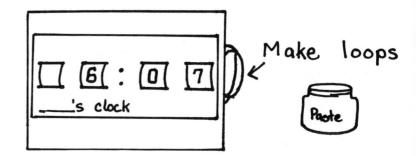

Make loops

_____'s clock

File Folder Directions

Astronaut's Day

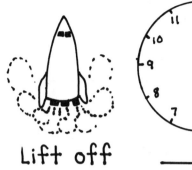 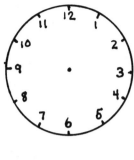

Lift off _____

Check instruments _____

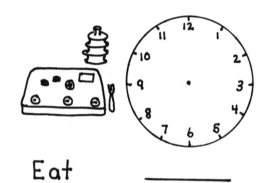

Eat _____

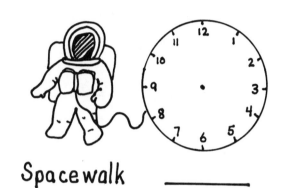

Spacewalk _____

Experiments _____

Exercise _____

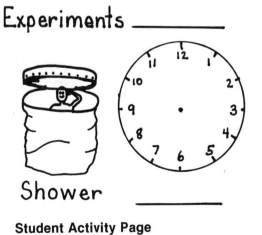

Shower _____

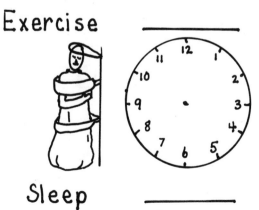

Sleep _____

Student Activity Page

171

Student's Clock

| 1 | 2 | : | 3 | 4 |

_____'s clock

paste	1	—
paste	2	0 9 8 7 6 5 4 3 2 1
paste	3	0 5 4 3 2 1
paste	4	0 9 8 7 6 5 4 3 2 1

Student Activity Page

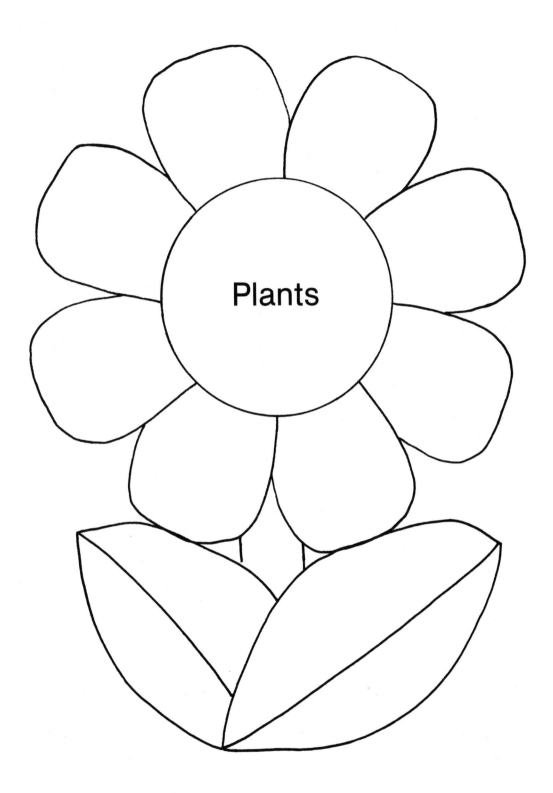

Plants

HOW DOES OUR GARDEN GROW?

Date _____

Dear Parent,

Our next set of learning centers will be about plants. We will emphasize parts of the plant, plant care, edible plants, and gardens.

Your child will measure the length of plant roots at the Happy Giant's Garden Center. He or she may want to measure other parts of plants at home.

At the Seeds Center your child will conduct a germination test. He or she will bring home a plastic bag that contains seeds rolled in a paper towel. Encourage the child to put the seeds in a warm place, keep them wet, and check them after one week.

Please send a facial tissue box as soon as possible for our vegetable patch center. The child will be making seed packages at this center.

The long-awaited Plant Show will be held on _____

_____ at _____.

On that day your child will have the opportunity to share his or her plant-care experience with the class. Please send the plant your child has been caring for during the past month at home (regardless of what it looks like). The child will also need his or her plant-care calendar to use as a reference in writing a plant story.

You are welcome to come to the Plant Show. I appreciate the help you have given your child with the plant project. Hopefully, he or she will continue to care for plants in your home or garden.

Sincerely,

_____

Your child's teacher

PLANT SHOW NEWS

Date _____

Dear Parent,

In one month our class will begin working in Plant Learning Centers. As a culminating activity of these learning centers we will have a Plant

Show on _____.

Each child will care for a plant at home and bring it to school for the Plant Show. Your child may care for a plant you already have in your home or start one from a seed, bulb, cutting, or sprout (such as a potato, onion, or carrot top).

Encourage your child to use the attached calendar to indicate the day he or she began to care for the plant, watering days, growth changes, and any other relevant information. On the day of the Plant Show your child will need to bring the calendar to school. He or she will then write a story about the plant, using the calendar as a reference.

The purpose of this plant-care activity is to (1) learn about the care and nature of plants, (2) encourage responsibility, and (3) develop a good sense of self-esteem.

Please send the calendar and the plant on the day of the Plant Show, regardless of the outcome of the plant-care experiment (we can learn from mistakes, too!).

I appreciate your help with this project. You are welcome to come to the Plant Show. Please return the attached Student Plant Care note tomorrow.

Sincerely,

_____
Your child's teacher

My Plant Care Calendar

Sunday	Monday	Tuesday	Wednesday	Thursday	Friday	Saturday

student name _____

plant name _____

return to school on _____

student plant care calendar

STUDENT PLANT CARE NOTE

Please return this Student Plant Care note on: _____.

    My child and I have discussed the home plant project. He/she will

care for _____, will use the calendar
                        type of plant

to record the plant care, and will return the calendar with the plant on the

day of the Plant Show _____.

My Plant

_____
Parent's signature

_____
Student's signature

GROUP ACTIVITY

The group activity for the Plants Learning Centers is a Plant Show. This requires advance preparation to ensure that your students will each have a plant to bring to the show. Parents should be sent the plant show news letter, calendar, and student plant care note at least one month before the Plant Show will be held.

BOARDWORK ACTIVITIES

1. Make fact cards about the flowers grown in your area.

2. Write plant riddles: "I give the plant support. I am the stalk of the plant. What am I?" (stem) You might ask students to draw pictures of stems they eat. Examples are celery and asparagus. "I live underground. I store food. I absorb moisture. What am I?" (root) Ask students to draw pictures of roots they eat. Examples are carrots, beets, and potatoes.

3. Write poems and nursery rhymes about plants on the chalkboard. The student copies them and illustrates them. Examples are "Peter, Peter, Pumpkin Eater" and "Mary, Mary, Quite Contrary."

4. Use 16 vegetable seed packages and have the student choose one or more packages.

   An older student can write about the vegetable (when to plant, where to plant, how to plant, its height, and so on) using the seed package as a reference.

   A younger student can write the name of the vegetable, draw a picture of the vegetable, and write a sentence about the vegetable.

5. Here are several dictionary–pictionary ideas using an eight-box format:

   a. Ask an older student to
      - Find eight plants that grow underground
      - Find eight plants that grow on vines
      - Find vegetables that grow in pods
      - Find fruits that have peels

   b. Ask a younger student to
      - Find eight vegetables
      - Find eight fruits

6. Develop a "What if?" class book. Each student writes a "What if?" plant question on 12-by-18-inch paper and illustrates it. You can then compile the stories in a class book. Some ideas are:
   - "What if a marigold had a cold?"
   - "What if a pussy willow were a pillow?"
   - "What if a rose had a nose?"
   - "What if a tulip had two lips?"
   - "What if a daffodil took a pill?"

7. Make flashcards using an eight-box format. Write eight fruit words on the chalkboard. The student copies the words on the front side of the paper. Then he or she cuts the paper apart to form eight word cards. The child draws the matching fruit picture on the back of the card.

8. Make plant bingo cards using a 16-box format. Write 16 plant words (root, stem, leaf, flower, seed, bulb, fruit, vegetable, and so on) on the chalkboard. The student copies the words in random order on the 16-box paper. Later in the day, play Bingo. You call the plant words and the students cover the words you call with paper markers. The winner needs to cover four words across, diagonally, horizontally, or vertically.

9. Write plant stories on the day of the Plant Show. The students write about their plants using their calendar as a reference.

PLANT CENTER MARKER

Distribute copies of the flower marker to the students. The students cut out their markers and place them near the Plant Learning Centers.

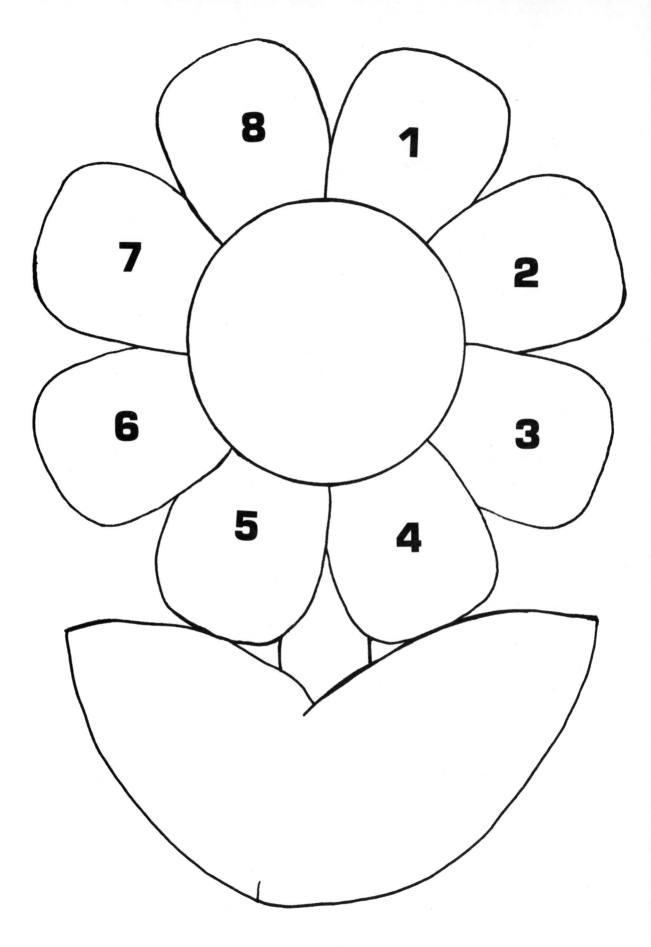

LEARNING CENTERS LIST

These learning centers are about plants, with emphasis on plant care, plant parts, vegetables, and flowers.

Happy Giant's Garden Center

(A bulletin board is used with this center.)

Content areas: Math, science, handwriting, reading

Skills: Linear measurement, matching, communicating

Activities:

1. Match the names to the roots.
2. Measure the roots and record measurements on the student activity page.

Parts of Plants Center

Content areas: Science, handwriting, reading

Skills: Observing, fine-motor coordination, matching

Activities:

1. Observe plants with a magnifying glass or microscope.
2. Write names of the parts of the plant on the overhead projector and the student activity page.

Plant Care Center

Content areas: Reading, handwriting, art

Skills: Listening, creative writing, creating

Activities:

1. Listen to the story about plant care.
2. Write a story about plant care.

Plants We Eat Center

Content areas: Reading, science, handwriting

Skills: Classifying, sorting, matching, communicating

Activities:

1. Sort the plant picture–word cards.
2. Write plant words and draw pictures of seeds.

Seeds Center

Content areas: Science, handwriting, art

Skills: Experimenting, observing, creating, communicating

Activities:

1. Make a germination test with four different kinds of seeds.
2. Make a seed picture.

Vegetable Patch Center

Content areas: Art, handwriting

Skills: Creating, fine-motor coordination

Activities:

1. Make a vegetable patch box.
2. Make vegetable seed packages.

Sunflower Center (Open-Ended Activity)

Content areas: Art, handwriting, teacher's choice

Skills: Creating, communicating, fine-motor coordination, teacher's choice

Activities:

1. Write the words on the strips.
2. Make a sunflower picture.

Flower Garden Center

Content areas: Art, handwriting

Skills: Creating, fine-motor coordination

Activities:

1. Write a poem.
2. Paint a flower garden.

TEACHER'S DIRECTIONS FOR THE HAPPY GIANT'S GARDEN CENTER

Content areas: Math, science, handwriting, reading

Skills: Linear measurement, matching, communicating

Materials needed:

Bulletin board
Copies of student activity page
Teacher-made plant word cards
Thumbtacks and container
Ruler
Crayons
Pencil

Materials preparation:

1. Prepare the "Happy Giant's Garden" bulletin board as shown here.

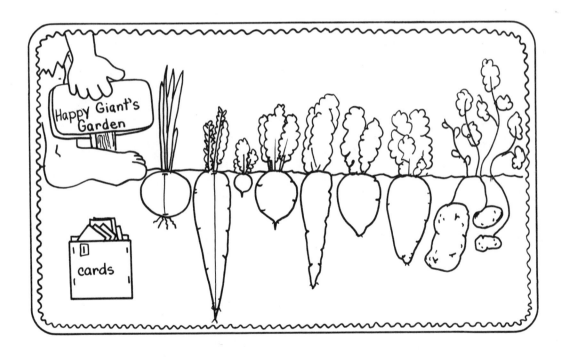

2. Make the plant word cards. Write the following words on 3-by-5-inch index cards: onion, carrot, radish, beet, parsnip, turnip, potato, and sweet potato. (Laminate the cards or cover them with clear Con-Tact paper.)

3. Provide a container for the cards.

Directions for file folder activities:

Activity 1

The student tacks the plant word cards to the matching plants on the bulletin board.

Activity 2

The student uses a ruler to measure the roots of the plants on the bulletin board. Then he or she records the measurements on the student activity page.

Optional Activity

You might have students use thumbs, coins, or other items to measure the roots. Ask students to estimate the length of the roots.

Happy Giant's Garden

1 Match the names to the roots.

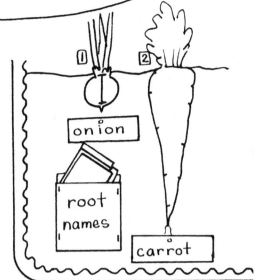

2 Measure the roots. Write the answers on the ditto.

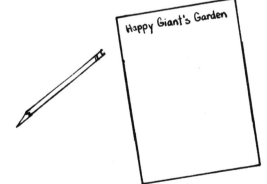

File Folder Directions

185

Happy Giant's Garden

[ruler drawing] How long is each root?

1. onion _____

2. carrot _____

3. radish _____

4. beet _____

5. parsnip _____

6. turnip _____

7. sweet potato _____

8. potato _____

These plants store food in their roots.

Name _____

TEACHER'S DIRECTIONS FOR THE PARTS OF PLANTS CENTER

Content areas: Science, handwriting, reading

Skills: Observing, fine-motor coordination, matching

Materials needed:

Copies of student activity page

Teacher-made transparency of student activity page

Marking pen for overhead transparency

Overhead projector and screen

Several live plants

Magnifying glass or dissecting microscope

Pencil

Crayons

Materials preparation:

Make a transparency of the student activity page on an acetate sheet to use on an overhead projector. If an overhead projector is unavailable, copy the student activity page plant diagram on the chalkboard. The student writes the names of the parts of the plant with chalk (referring to the student activity page).

Directions for file folder activities:

Activity 1

The student observes plants with a magnifying glass or microscope.

Activity 2

The student writes the names of the parts of the plant on the overhead projector transparency with a marking pen.

Activity 3

The student uses a pencil to write the names of the parts of the plant on the student activity page. He or she then colors the plant picture.

Optional Activity

An older student may write the functions of the parts of the plant using references.

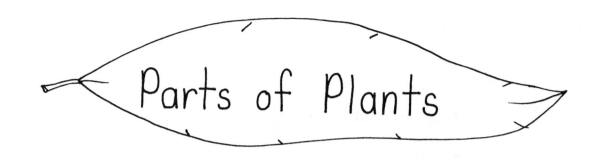

Parts of Plants

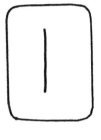 **1** Look at the plants.

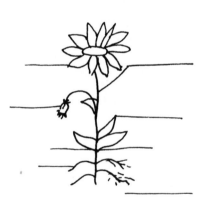 **2** Write the parts of the plants.

3 Now do ditto.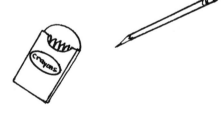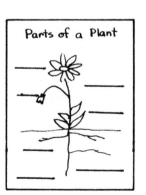

File Folder Directions

Parts of a Plant

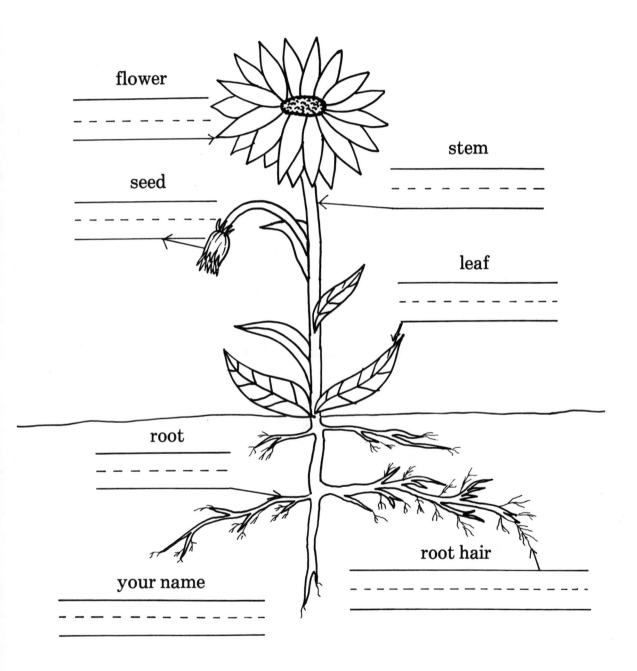

flower

_____

— — — — — — — —

stem

_____

— — — — — — — —

seed

_____

— — — — — — — —

leaf

_____

— — — — — — — —

root

_____

— — — — — — — —

root hair

_____

— — — — — — — — — —

your name

_____

— — — — — — — —

Student Activity Page

189

TEACHER'S DIRECTIONS FOR THE PLANT CARE CENTER

Content areas: Reading, handwriting, art

Skills: Listening, creative writing, creating

Materials needed:

Copies of student activity page

Pencil

Crayons

Tape recorder

Cassette tape

A book about plant care such as: Zion, Gene, *The Plant Sitter*, Harper and Row, New York, 1959; Krauss, Ruth, *The Carrot Seed*, Scholastic Book Services, New York, 1971.

Materials preparation:

Prepare a cassette tape of the book.

Directions for file folder activities:

Activity 1

The student listens to the cassette tape of the book.

Activity 2

The student writes a creative story about plant care on the student activity page referring to the vocabulary listed. The student may illustrate the story on the back of the student activity page.

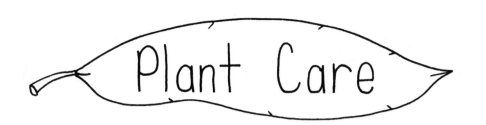
Plant Care

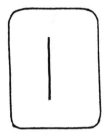
1 Listen to the book.

2 Do the ditto.

Plant Care

alive   feed
water grow   fertilizer
  plant blossom root daily
weed   care
  seed cut sunlight
          house

plant sitter's name:

_____

Student Activity Page

TEACHER'S DIRECTIONS FOR THE PLANTS WE EAT CENTER

Content areas: Reading, science, handwriting

Skills: Classifying, sorting, matching, communicating

Materials needed:

Teacher-made example of plants paper

Teacher-made plant picture–word cards

Box

One sheet of 12-by-18-inch paper per student

Crayons

Pencil

Materials preparation:

1. To make the example of plants paper, fold a 12-by-18-inch paper into fourths. Use a pencil to line the folds and write the four category words: roots, leaves, seeds, and fruits.

2. To make the plant picture–word cards, prepare four plant–picture word cards (on 3-by-5-inch index cards) for each category.

   a. Roots (radish, potato, carrot, onion, beet)

   b. Leaves (lettuce, cabbage, spinach, dandelion, turnip)

   c. Seeds (pumpkin, corn, pea, bean, peanut)

   d. Fruits (peach, plum, cherry, pear, apple)

   (You may want to use seed catalogs for pictures.)

3. Provide a container for the cards.

4. Prepare a "Plants We Eat" box as pictured on the file folder directions page.

Directions for file folder activities:

Activity 1

The student sorts the plant picture cards into the "Plants We Eat" box (four cards per category).

Activity 2

The student prepares a 12-by-18-inch paper according to your example. The student draws the four pictures in each category referring to the plant picture cards. An older student may also write the words in each category.

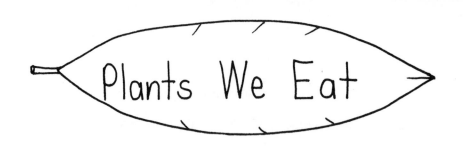

Plants We Eat

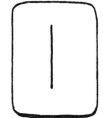

1 Sort the plants.

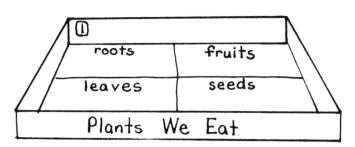

roots	fruits
leaves	seeds

Plants We Eat

plant cards

2 Now draw four pictures for each group on your paper.

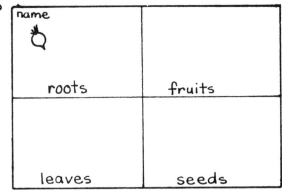

name

roots	fruits
leaves	seeds

File Folder Directions

194

TEACHER'S DIRECTIONS FOR THE SEEDS CENTER

Content areas: Science, handwriting, art

Skills: Experimenting, observing, creating, communicating

Materials needed:

Teacher-made paper towel example

Teacher-made index card example

Four different kinds of seeds (examples are corn, pea, lima bean, pumpkin)

Container for seeds

Container with water

One paper towel per student

One plastic bag per student

One index card per student

Masking tape

Pencil

Glue

One sheet of 8-by-8-inch posterboard per student

Materials preparation:

1. To make the paper towel example, fold a paper towel into eight boxes and draw lines on the folds with a pencil. Write the names of the four seeds in the bottom row of boxes (one per box). Glue four seeds of each kind onto the matching boxes.

2. To make the index card example, write the following information on an index card:

---

name   date

I need to keep this bag in a warm place.

I need to keep it wet.

I need to open it in one week.

(You may prefer to make a ditto copy of this information for younger students.)

Directions for file folder activities:

Activity 1

1. The student prepares a paper towel according to your example, but does not glue on seeds.
2. He or she lays four seeds onto each of the four boxes.
3. The student folds the top half of the towel over the seeds in the bottom half.
4. The student gets the towel wet with water.
5. He or she puts the towel into a plastic bag.
6. He or she copies your index card.
7. He or she then tapes the index card onto the plastic bag.
   (The student takes the bag home, follows the instructions, and discusses his or her observation in class the following week.)

Activity 2

The student glues several seeds onto posterboard to form a seed picture.

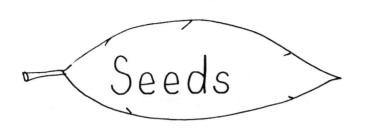

Seeds

1 Make a
germination test. Wet it.

Put it in a bag.

Wait a week. Open it. What will you see?

2 Make a seed picture.

Seeds

by name

TEACHER'S DIRECTIONS FOR THE VEGETABLE PATCH CENTER

Content areas: Art, handwriting

Skills: Creating, fine-motor coordination

Materials needed:

Two copies of student activity page per student

Teacher-made vegetable patch box

One facial tissue box per student

Six pipe cleaners per student

Nail

Permanent brown marking pen

Pencil

Crayons

Scissors

Glue

Materials preparation:

To make the vegetable patch box, use a permanent brown marking pen to color the bottom and the sides of a facial tissue box. Turn the box upside down and poke six nail holes in it as pictured in the file folder directions.

Directions for file folder activities:

Activity 1

The student prepares a box according to your example.

Activity 2

1. The student colors, writes six vegetable seed names, and cuts out the seed packages on the student activity pages.
2. He or she folds and glues the packages onto pipe cleaners.
3. He or she inserts the pipe cleaners into the holes in the box.

Optional Activities

Older students may arrange packages in alphabetical order. They may write additional information (such as growing time) on the seed packages using a seed catalog as a reference.

Vegetable Patch

1 Make the patch from a box.

Color it.

Punch 6 holes

2 Make the seed packages.
Put on pictures.
Write its name.

Glue onto a pipe cleaner.

File Folder Directions

199

name

name

name

TEACHER'S DIRECTIONS FOR THE SUNFLOWER CENTER

Content areas: Art, handwriting, teacher's choice

Skills: Creating, communicating, fine-motor coordination, teacher's choice

Materials needed:

Eight strips of 1½-by-8½-inch yellow construction paper per student

One sheet of 12-by-18-inch blue construction paper per student

One sheet of 5½-by-9-inch green construction paper per student

One sheet of 4-by-4-inch black construction paper per student

Three-inch circular pattern

Sunflower seeds and container

Scissors

Glue

Pencil

Materials preparation:

1. Determine the skill to be reinforced or reviewed, such as spelling words or reading vocabulary.
2. Provide references, such as a spelling book or reading book, or make a reference chart of the words.
3. Optional: You may want to make a sunflower example as shown on the file folder directions page.

Directions for file folder activities:

Activity 1

The student writes the words on the yellow construction paper strips. Then he or she glues each strip to form a loop.

Activity 2

1. The student uses a pencil to trace a circular pattern on black construction paper.
2. He or she cuts out the circle of black paper and glues it on the blue construction paper.
3. He or she covers the black circle by gluing sunflower seeds onto it.
4. The student then draws and cuts the leaves and stem out of green construction paper.
5. He or she glues the leaves and stem onto the blue construction paper.
6. Finally, the student glues the yellow word strips onto the blue paper to form a sunflower.

Sunflower

1 Write the words on the strips.

Loop them.

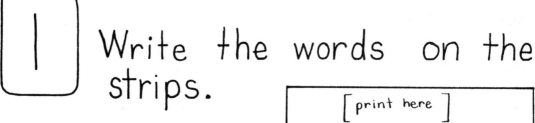

[print here]

2 Make a sunflower center.

Glue on seeds.

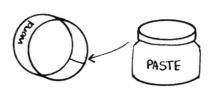

Make stem and leaves.

Paste the parts on the paper.

Can you read your words?

name

File Folder Directions

TEACHER'S DIRECTIONS FOR THE FLOWER GARDEN CENTER

Content areas: Art, handwriting

Skills: Creating, fine-motor coordination

Materials needed:

Easel

Paint

Paintbrushes

One sheet of 18-by-24-inch paper per student

Scissors

Pencil

Teacher-made example of poem

Materials preparation:

Write a poem about flowers. Here is an example by Carol Poppe:

"Row by Row"
Plant the seeds,
Row by row,
Rain and sun
Will help them grow,
Bringing flowers,
Row by row.

You may prefer to make a posterboard triangle pattern for the students to trace on painting paper.

Directions for file folder activities:

Activity 1

1. The student draws and cuts out a triangle-shaped piece of paper.
2. The student writes a poem around the sides of the triangle-shaped paper referring to your example.

Activity 2

The student paints rows of flowers on the opposite side of the triangle-shaped paper.

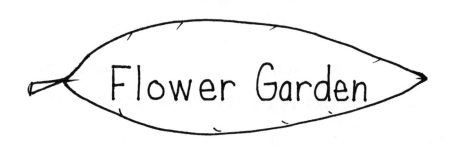

Flower Garden

Write the poem around the paper.

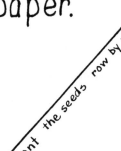

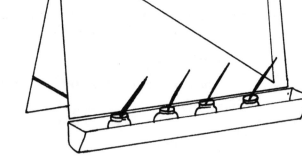
Now paint a flower garden.

Dinosaurs

DINOSAUR DAYS

Date _____

Dear Parent,

Watch out! Dinosaurs are making a return from extinction—at least in our classroom! We will be learning about dinosaurs during the next two weeks.

In addition to participating in the learning center activities, your child will learn a simple fact about dinosaurs at each center. He or she will copy it on a strip of paper, read it, form it into a loop, and staple it to a gigantic Stegosaurus on our bulletin board.

Each day during the boardwork period your child will write a variety of information about dinosaurs.

At one of the centers your child will make a diorama of dinosaur life. Please send an empty shoe box or facial tissue box with your child as soon as possible.

During the next two weeks your child is welcome to bring books, puzzles, games, fossils, and other things that relate to the dinosaur theme. Make sure your child's name appears somewhere on these items.

If possible, you can extend your child's interest in prehistoric animals

by taking him or her to the _____ Museum. It is located at

_____. The hours are _____. Admission is _____.
You are welcome, as always, to visit us and see our learning centers in

action between the hours of _____ and _____.
Thank you for your continued support.

Sincerely,

_____
Your child's teacher

GROUP ACTIVITIES

As an introduction to the "Dinosaur Stew" group activity, you may want to read the following book: Brown, Marcia, *Stone Soup*, Scribner's, New York, 1947. This folk tale is about hungry soldiers who trick people into contributing food to make a soup from a stone.

A class discussion should be held to encourage ideas about using a fossil to make "Dinosaur Stew." (Emphasize the fact that since dinosaurs are extinct, there is no dinosaur meat, only fossils.) Some discussion questions might be: What other ingredients could you put in stew? What day would be best to make stew at school? What utensils would you need to cook stew? How may parents help us?

Following the discussion, send a letter to parents requesting help, ingredients, and a sack lunch for their child on the day "Dinosaur Stew" is made.

The parents who will help with the project can bring in utensils such as sharp knives, spoons for stirring, ladles, pots, hot plates, hot pads, or whatever else your class needs for this project.

The Dinosaur Stew activity can be handled in a quiet, efficient way with the help of two or three parents. During the morning the students will follow the regular morning rotation schedule (reading, boardwork, learning center, and seatwork). The parents will work with one group of students during their seatwork time (approximately half an hour) at a prearranged area.

On the morning that you make Dinosaur Stew, put a large fossilized stone (large enough not to be mistaken for the other stew ingredients) in a large pot of water. Add two bay leaves and chicken bouillon (one per three cups of water). Bring the water to a boil.

The students can wash, peel, and cut carrots, potatoes, celery, tomatoes, hot dogs, and onions and put them into the pot with the fossilized stone. Simmer the stew until the vegetables are tender. Then thicken the stew by adding a mixture of flour and water. Remove the fossilized stone and serve the Dinosaur Stew.

In addition to the Dinosaur Stew, each child will have a sack lunch and milk to complete his or her nutritional requirements, as requested in the parent letter.

Optional activities: Make place mats prior to eating lunch, write experience stories about the Dinosaur Stew project, and write parent thank-you letters.

DINOSAUR STEW

Date _____

Dear Parent,

    As you know, we have been learning about dinosaurs. On _____
                                                                                         day

we will make "Dinosaur Stew." We will use a fossilized stone for the dinosaur part. On that day please send with your child a raw vegetable or any other items from the list below. Also send a sack lunch for your child.

    You may check any items from the list below. I will contact you later about the specific items I would like you to send.

    Please fill in the lower portion of this note if you would be able to help us prepare

this yummy project on _____ at _____. I will notify you later
                                day   time

regarding the utensils I would like you to bring.

    Thank you for your continued support.

Sincerely,

Your child's teacher

------------------------------ **cut along line** ------------------------------

_____
      Child's name

    I would be willing to send in any *one* of the following items that I have checked:

_____ carrot	_____ tomato	_____ onion	_____ 30 paper cups
_____ potato	_____ hot dog	_____ one cup of flour	_____ 30 paper bowls
_____ celery rib	_____ bay leaf	_____ chicken bouillon	_____ 30 plastic spoons
			_____ 1 gallon of milk

_____ Yes, I would be willing to help the children make dinosaur stew.

signed _____ phone _____

Please return this note by _____ so I can contact you for definite arrangements.

BOARDWORK ACTIVITIES

1. Write fact cards about dinosaurs. Use a "Dinosaur of the Day" theme. Write facts about a different dinosaur each day on the chalkboard. The student copies the facts and illustrates them. (You may want to use a commercial set of dinosaur pictures as a reference.)

2. Write dinosaur riddles. Students can write and illustrate their own riddles, too. A good book to motivate this activity is: Sterne, Noelle, *Tyrannosaurus Wrecks*, Thomas Y. Crowell, New York, 1979.

3. Make word bank charts about various traits of dinosaurs, such as plant eater, meat eater, fighter, spikes, horns, length, weight, height, and so on. Students use the charts as a reference for creative writing.

4. Make dinosaur puppets out of a variety of materials. Write a story about the puppet.

5. Create poems. You may want to write poems on the chalkboard for the students to copy and illustrate. A good book of verses is: Cole, William, *Dinosaurs and beasts of yore*, William Collins, New York, 1979.

6. Write "Brontosaurus" on the chalkboard. The student makes a list of all the words he or she can find in Brontosaurus. Examples are sat, bat, rat, ran, tan, ban, ton, son, tub, rub, sub. The student writes and illustrates stories and rhymes using these words.

7. Make a class dinosaur shape book.

8. Have the student write a letter to a parent, teacher, or another student about the Dinosaur Learning Center activities. He or she may design a dinosaur stamp to place on an envelope and then write the address on the envelope.

9. Write experience stories about the group activity "Dinosaur Stew."

DINOSAUR CENTER MARKER

Distribute copies of the dinosaur marker to the students. The students cut out their markers and place them near the Dinosaur Learning Centers.

Name _____

LEARNING CENTERS LIST

These learning centers emphasize eight facts about dinosaurs.

What If I Lived with a Dinosaur Center

Content areas: Reading, art, handwriting

Skills: Listening, creating, creative writing

Activities:

1. Listen to a story about a dinosaur.
2. Write a story, "If I lived with a dinosaur . . ." and illustrate it.

Where Are All the Dinosaurs Center

Content area: handwriting

Skill: Fine-motor coordination

Activities:

1. Use a paintbrush and water to write "dinosaurs disappeared" on the chalkboard.
2. Trace and write words on the student activity page.

How Were Dinosaurs Born Center (Open-Ended Activity)

Content area: Teacher's choice

Skills: Matching, fine-motor coordination, teacher's choice

Activities:

1. Play a teacher-made egg game.
2. Make an original egg game.

Who Saw a Dinosaur Center

Content area: Art

Skills: Creating, fine-motor coordination

Activities:

1. Make a dinosaur picture.
2. Make a dinosaur pin design.

What Color Were Dinosaurs Center

Content areas: Handwriting, art

Skills: Creating, fine-motor coordination

Activities:

1. Trace a dinosaur pattern and copy a sentence about it.
2. Glue rice or macaroni on the dinosaur outline.

What Happened to Dinosaur Bones Center

Content areas: Reading and science

Skills: Listening, matching, observing

Activities:

1. Listen to a story about fossils.
2. Make leaf and shell prints in clay.
3. Match a teacher-made puzzle.
4. Match fossil pictures and words on a student activity page.

How Much Did Dinosaurs Weigh Center

Content areas: Math, science, reading

Skills: Measuring weight, sorting, matching, classifying

Activities:

1. Sort and match weight cans on square mats.
2. Use a balance scale to weigh dinosaurs with metric units.
3. Color the student activity page.

What Was the World Like When Dinosaurs Lived Center

Content area: Art

Skills: Creating, fine-motor coordination

Activities:

1. Color the background in a box.
2. Color, cut, and paste pictures from the student activity page into the box to make a diorama.

TEACHER'S DIRECTIONS FOR THE
OVERALL DINOSAUR LEARNING CENTERS

On the top of each file folder directions page is a question about dinosaurs. The center's activities relate to that question. At each center is a container of 2-by-9-inch blank construction paper strips matching the color of the question on the file folder. You should color in these questions before you laminate the student file folder directions. Each question should be a different color.

The first thing a student does upon arriving at the center is write an answer to the question on the corresponding color of 2-by-9-inch paper, then proceed with the other center activities. The question in the following illustration is "How were dinosaurs born?"

When the student moves to the reading table, he or she takes the strip and finished center work. The student reads his or her answer at the reading table to the other members of the reading group.

Sample answers appear on the bulletin board on the same color-coded paper. Loop and staple the student's answer strips daily to the giant outline of a dinosaur on the bulletin board, as shown here.

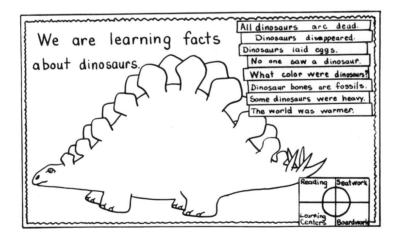

At the end of eight days of dinosaur centers, the dinosaur on the bulletin board is filled with colorful loops and the students are filled with knowledge about dinosaurs.

TEACHER'S DIRECTIONS FOR THE
WHAT IF I LIVED WITH A DINOSAUR CENTER

Content areas: Reading, art, handwriting

Skills: Listening, creating, creative writing

Materials needed:

Copies of student activity page

Pencil

Crayons

Tape recorder

Cassette tape

A book about a child and a dinosaur such as: Hoff, Syd, *Danny and the Dinosaur*, Harper & Row, New York, 1958

Materials preparation:

Prepare a cassette tape. Include the following items:

1. Explain the difference between real and imaginary stories. Stress that the story at this center is an imaginary one because all dinosaurs are dead.
2. Read the story.
3. Give directions for the student activity page.

Directions for file folder activities:

Activity 1

The student listens to the cassette tape of the book.

Activity 2

The student writes a creative story on the subject, "If I lived with a dinosaur . . ." on the student activity page. The student draws a picture of him- or herself with the dinosaur in the cloud on the student activity page.

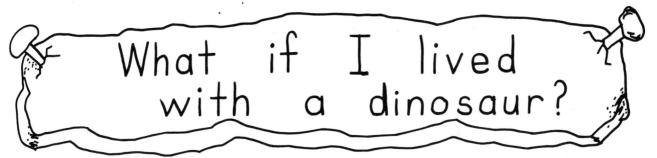

What if I lived with a dinosaur?

It is fun to think about living with a real dinosaur, but now they are all dead.

1 Listen to the book.

2 Do ditto.

File Folder Directions

If

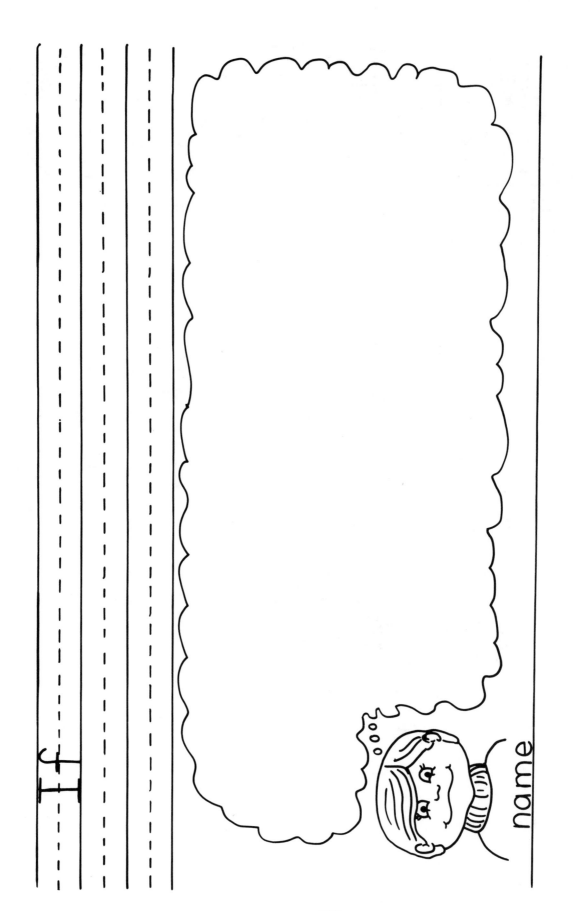

name

TEACHER'S DIRECTIONS FOR THE
WHERE ARE ALL THE DINOSAURS CENTER

Content area: Handwriting

Skills: Fine-motor coordination

Materials needed:

Chalkboard

Copies of student activity page

Plastic cup with a small amount of water

Paintbrush

Pencil

Crayons

Materials preparation:

1. Use chalk to write the words, "Dinosaurs disappeared" on the chalkboard. Write "1" and "2" as pictured on the file folder directions.

2. Set a plastic cup with a small amount of water in it and a paintbrush on the chalk ledge.

Directions for file folder activities:

Activity 1

The student dips a paintbrush into the water and "paints" the words "dinosaurs disappeared" next to numbers 1 and 2 on the chalkboard, referring to your example. (The words written with water will disappear, just like the dinosaurs did long ago. The chalkboard will be clean in time for the next student who uses the center.)

Activity 2

The student uses a pencil to trace then write words on the student activity page. He or she colors the pictures on the student activity page.

Where are all the dinosaurs?

All the dinosaurs disappeared.

 **1** Paint on the board.

Dinosaurs disappeared.

2 Do ditto.

name

D
d

File Folder Directions

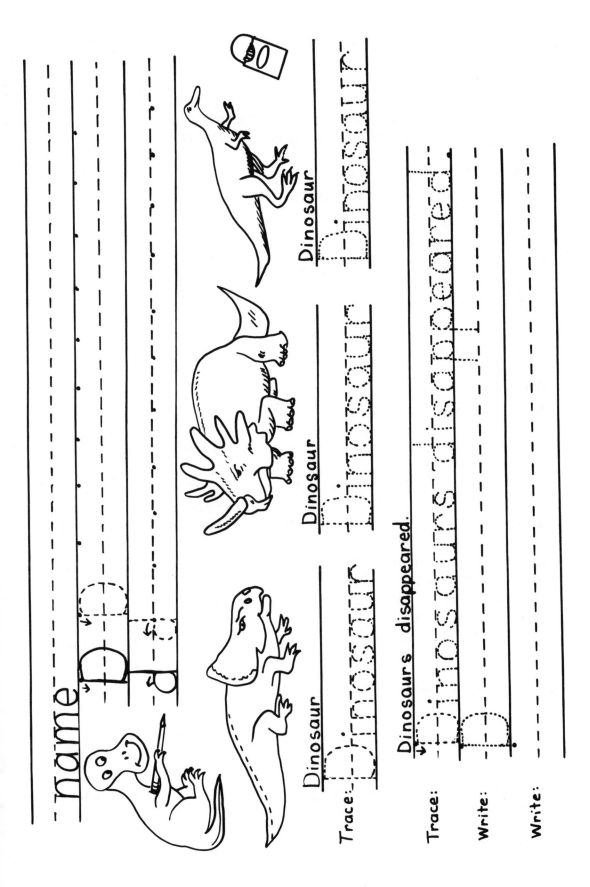

name

Dinosaur

Dinosaur

Dinosaur

Trace: Dinosaur

Dinosaurs disappeared.

Trace: Dinosaurs disappeared.

Write: D

Write:

TEACHER'S DIRECTIONS FOR THE
HOW WERE DINOSAURS BORN CENTER

Content area: Teacher's choice

Skills: Matching, fine-motor coordination, teacher's choice

Materials needed:

Teacher-made egg-matching game

Two pieces of 12-by-18-inch oaktag or heavy paper

One sheet of 12-by-18-inch construction paper per student

Pencil

Scissors

One envelope per student

Materials preparation:

Before making the egg-matching game, determine a skill you wish to reinforce or review. Some ideas are contractions, upper- and lowercase letters, numerals and objects, color words and colors, and math problems and answers.

1. Cut out the egg pattern on the teacher egg game direction page. Trace around the pattern eight times on a piece of oaktag. Write a different word or math problem on each egg. (For contractions, for example, write "I'll" on the top half of an egg and "I will" on the bottom half.) Cut each egg apart differently to make the game self-checking.

2. Make an egg pattern for the students to use. (You may want to make additional egg patterns to keep handy.)

3. Use a file folder to make a Dinosaur Eggs envelope, as pictured on the teacher egg game direction page.

4. Laminate the eggs and the envelope or cover them with clear Con-Tact paper.

Directions for file folder activities:

Activity 1

The student plays the teacher-made egg game.

Activity 2

The student makes his or her own egg game referring to your sample game. The student puts the game in an envelope.

Egg Game

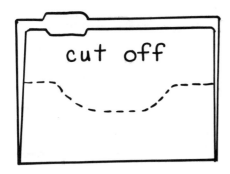

cut off

Dinosaur Eggs

Make 8 eggs

pattern

Teacher Directions

How were dinosaurs born?

Dinosaurs laid eggs.

1 Match the eggs.

Dinosaur Eggs

2 Make your own game.

Trace the egg pattern 8 times.

Write on the eggs.

Cut the eggs.

TEACHER'S DIRECTIONS FOR THE
WHO SAW A DINOSAUR CENTER

Content area: Art

Skills: Creating, fine-motor coordination

Materials needed:

Copies of student activity page

Easel

Paint

Paintbrushes

Paper

One sheet of 9-by-12-inch construction paper per student

Straight pins

Stapler and staples

Carpet sample

Materials preparation:

1. Prepare the student activity page in the following way for a pin design: Place the student activity page on top of a piece of construction paper. Staple the top corners of both papers together. Insert a straight pin through the top of the student activity page.

2. Provide a carpet sample at this center to protect the desk top from pin scratches.

Directions for file folder activities:

Activity 1

The student paints a picture of a dinosaur.

Activity 2

The student makes a pin design picture.

1. He or she removes the straight pin from the top of the student activity page.

2. He or she uses the pin to punch holes through the outline of Brontosaurus on the student activity page. (Be sure the student does this work over the carpet sample.)

3. He or she removes the student activity page from the construction paper. (The outline of Brontosaurus will be visible on the construction paper.)

# Who saw a dinosaur?

No one ever saw a dinosaur. Dinosaurs lived before people did.

 **1** Paint a picture of a dinosaur.

2 Make a pin design. Keep a carpet under your design when you work.

File Folder Directions

name
Brontosaurus

Student Activity Page

TEACHER'S DIRECTIONS FOR THE
WHAT COLORS WERE DINOSAURS CENTER

Content areas: Handwriting, art

Skills: Creating, fine-motor coordination

Materials needed:

Teacher-made dinosaur patterns

One sheet of 9-by-12-inch oaktag per student

Two cups of rice per 30 students

Container and lid for rice

Tweezers

Glue

Pencil

Crayons

Envelope

Materials preparation:

1. To make the dinosaur patterns, ditto a copy of the teacher pattern directions. Cut out the patterns and put them in an envelope. (Laminate the patterns or cover them with clear Con-Tact paper.)

2. Color the rice using the following recipe for 30 students:
   a. Put three tablespoons of rubbing alcohol and a few drops of food coloring in a quart jar.
   b. Add two cups of rice.
   c. Put a lid on the jar.
   d. Shake the jar until the rice is colored.
   e. Spread the rice on paper to dry overnight.
   f. Daily, put a small amount of the rice in a small container with a lid on it at the center table.

Directions for file folder activities:

Activity 1

1. The student traces one of the dinosaur patterns on oaktag.
2. He or she copies the sentence from the pattern on the bottom of the oaktag.
3. He or she colors the background for the picture.

Activity 2

1. The student removes the lid from the rice container.
2. He or she takes one teaspoon of rice and spreads it on the lid.
3. He or she spreads glue in a thin line (approximately 2 inches) along a small portion of the dinosaur outline.
4. He or she uses tweezers to pick up one grain of rice at a time and place it on the glued outline. The student continues to glue and place rice on the dinosaur outline until it is covered.
5. The student lays the finished picture at a prearranged area to dry.

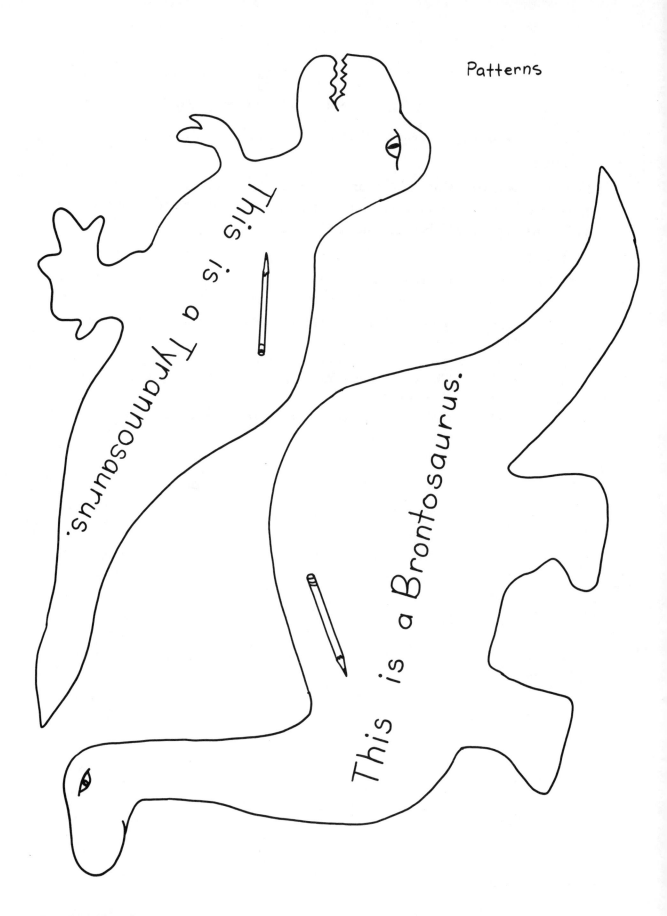

This is a Tyrannosaurus.

This is a Brontosaurus.

Teacher Directions

What color were dinosaurs?

No one knows what color dinosaurs were.
We have only found fossils, not real skin.

1 Trace a pattern.
Copy the sentence.
Color background.

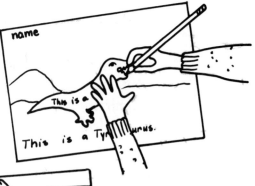

dinosaur patterns

2 Put on glue over some of the line.
Put on rice.

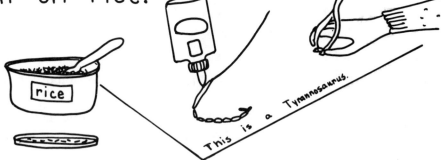

What a funny color for a dinosaur!

File Folder Directions

TEACHER'S DIRECTIONS FOR THE
WHAT HAPPENED TO DINOSAUR BONES CENTER

Content areas: Reading, science

Skills: Listening, matching, observing

Materials needed:

Copies of student activity page

Teacher-made matching puzzle cards

Container for puzzle cards

One envelope per student

One ball of clay per student (approximately 2 inches diameter)

Container and lid for clay

Magnifying glass

Plastic leaf

Shell

A collection of fossils or fossil pictures

Crayons

Pencil

Tape recorder

Cassette tape

Book about fossils such as Aliki, *Fossils Tell of Long Ago*, Thomas Y. Crowell, New York, 1972.

Materials preparation:

1. Display a collection of fossils or fossil pictures at this center.
2. To prepare a cassette tape:
   a. Read the book about fossils.
   b. Give directions for observing the fossil collection or pictures with a magnifying glass.
   c. Give directions for making an imprint of the plastic leaf and shell in clay. (Press the leaf on a flattened piece of clay. Press the shell in another flattened piece of clay.)
3. To make the puzzle cards:
   a. Run a ditto of the teacher puzzle direction page on oaktag.
   b. Color and cut apart each of the puzzle cards in a different way to make the cards self-checking. (Laminate the puzzle cards or cover them with clear Con-Tact paper.)
   c. Put the cards in a container at the center.

Directions for file folder activities:

Activity 1

The student listens to the cassette tape of the book.

Activity 2

1. The student observes the collection of fossils or fossil pictures with a magnifying glass.
2. He or she makes imprints of the shell and plastic leaf in clay according to the taped directions.
3. The student puts the clay imprints in an envelope.

Activity 3

The student matches the teacher-made puzzle cards.

Activity 4

The student uses a pencil to draw lines matching fossil words and pictures on the student activity page. He or she may color the fossil pictures.

footprint

teeth

leaf

trilobite

bone

shell

What happened to dinosaur bones?

Some dinosaur bones, plants, and other animals changed into stone called fossils.

1. Listen to the book.

2. Make imprints in the clay. → leaf   shell

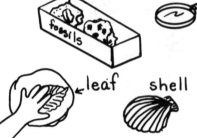

3. Match puzzle.

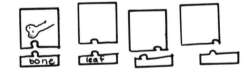

4. Do ditto.

Match the word to the fossil.

bone

leaf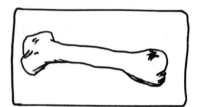

footprint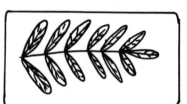

shell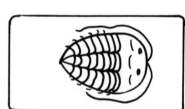

teeth

trilobite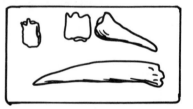

name_____

TEACHER'S DIRECTIONS FOR THE
HOW MUCH DID DINOSAURS WEIGH CENTER

Content areas: Math, science, reading

Skills: Measuring weight, sorting, matching, classifying

Materials needed:

Copies of student activity page

Teacher-made matching weight game

Balance scale

Plastic toy dinosaurs (10 or more in various sizes)

Container for the toy dinosaurs

Metric weights (1 to 20 grams)

Container for weights

Crayons

Pencil

Materials preparation:

1. To make the matching weight game, you will need:

   Eight identical opaque containers with lids (for instance, plastic catsup bottles, potato chip cans)

   Plaster of Paris

   Four pieces of 8-by-8-inch oaktag

   Permanent marking pen

   Box for containers

2. Fill pairs of containers with equal amounts of plaster of Paris: two containers are one-eighth full, two containers are half full, two containers are completely full, and two containers are empty.

3. Glue or tape lids on the containers so the student cannot visually check for differences in amounts of plaster of Paris.

4. Use a marking pen to trace the outlines of a pair of containers on each of the four squares of oaktag. (Laminate or cover the squares with clear Con-Tact paper.)

Directions for file folder activities:

Activity 1

The student sorts, matches, and places the identical-weight containers onto the square oaktag mats.

Activity 2

The student weighs toy dinosaurs with metric weights on the balance scale. (An older student may want to put dinosaurs in order from lightest to heaviest.)

Activity 3

The student completes the student activity page.

How much did dinosaurs weigh?

Some dinosaurs were very heavy.
Some were light and bird-like.

1 Match the cans.

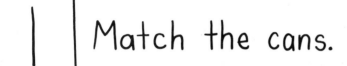

2 Use the scale.

3 Do ditto.

File Folder Directions

Spot the Dinosaur

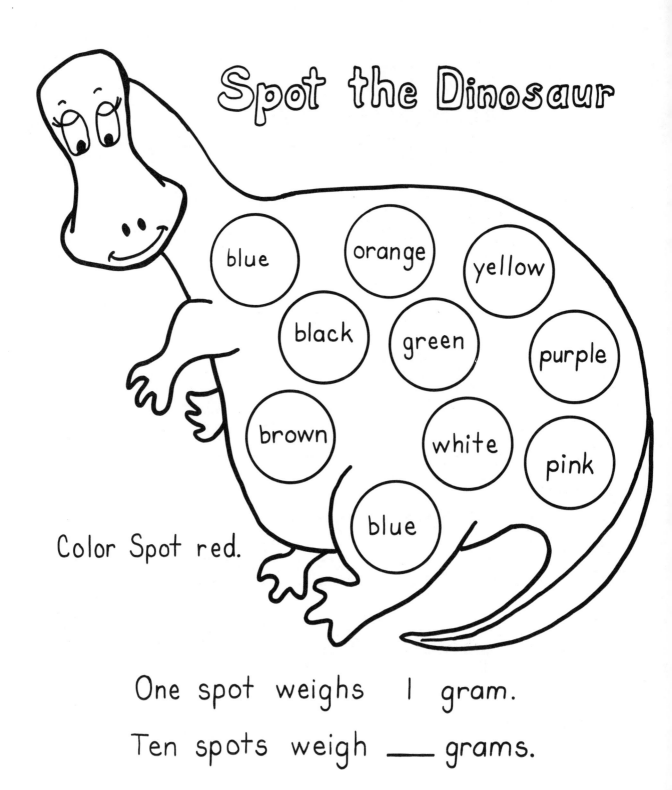

blue   orange   yellow

black   green

purple

brown   white

pink

blue

Color Spot red.

One spot weighs 1 gram.

Ten spots weigh ___ grams.

Name _____

TEACHER'S DIRECTIONS FOR THE
WHAT WAS THE WORLD LIKE WHEN DINOSAURS LIVED CENTER

Content area: Art

Skills: Creating, fine-motor coordination

Materials needed:

Copies of student activity page

One shoe box or facial tissue box per student

Green and blue broad-tip marking pens

Crayons

Scissors

Paste

Materials preparation:

You may want to make an example diorama in a shoe box with a few pictures from the student activity page pasted in it.

Directions for file folder activities:

Activity 1

The student uses the blue and green marking pens to make the sky and grass background inside the shoe box.

Activity 2

The student colors and cuts out pictures on the student activity page.

Activity 3

The student folds the pictures on the dotted lines and pastes them to the bottom of the shoe box to create a diorama.

What was the world like when dinosaurs lived?

The world was warmer when dinosaurs were alive.

1 Make blue sky.
Make green grass.

2 Color and cut the ditto.

3 Paste them into the box.

File Folder Directions

Student Activity Page